PRAISE FOR *SUCCESSFUL WOMAN'S GUIDE TO WORKING SMART*

"**THIS IS A** watershed workplace handbook for women—a serious corporate leadership success guide written by a serious author with the business battle scars to prove her points. And it's a handbook for men in the workplace because it reveals (sometimes painfully) the barriers that men (sometimes unknowingly) put in the way of their women colleagues. Absolutely a must-read for anyone in the workplace."

> —*J. Stephen Lanning, Executive Director, National Association of Business Coaches*

"**WHAT A BOOK!** It integrates sound advice on professional growth and career management with tools for achieving inner harmony. The result is a book of considerable importance to any working woman."

> —*Martin Yate, author of the "Knock 'Em Dead" books*

"**FROM CONCEPT TO** application, the real-life stories and exercises helped me reflect on my strengths and determine areas that need improvement. I plan on sharing this book with my friends and co-workers who are also striving to improve themselves professionally and personally."

> —*Rebecca Pille, Manager, Corporate Development Services, National Security Administration*

"**CAITLIN WILLIAMS** is very inspiring. She has a knowing quality for observing how people work. Her book is a must-read for all career women."

> —*Angie Yepez-Carrillo, World Wide Manager, Manufacturing & Development, Solectron*

"**THIS BOOK SEGMENTS** the elements of success, presenting them in manageable chunks easy to apply to your life and work. Caitlin Williams delineates the 'what' and 'how' of the Ten Strengths so clearly that we can easily create a workable self-development plan."

> —*Andrea Williams, Chair, Research & Education Committee, Women's Vision Foundation*

"**SUCCESSFUL WOMAN'S GUIDE** to *Working Smart* will be every working woman's 'bible' for success and for meeting those challenges we women face every day."

> —*Barbara A. Garrison, President, Federally Employed Women, Inc., Okinawa, Japan*

"**IF YOU ARE** longing to do what you love and love what you do, this book is for you. Solid, researched wisdom combines with practical, useable tools—first-class material with which to enhance your life!"

> —*Glenna Salsbury, professional speaker; past President, National Speakers Association; author of The Art of the Fresh Start*

SUCCESSFUL WOMAN'S
GUIDE TO

WORKING
SMART

SUCCESSFUL WOMAN'S GUIDE TO

WORKING SMART

TEN STRENGTHS THAT MATTER MOST

CAITLIN WILLIAMS

Davies-Black Publishing
Palo Alto, California

Published by Davies-Black Publishing, an imprint of Consulting Psychologists Press, Inc., 3803 East Bayshore Road, Palo Alto, CA 94303; 800-624-1765.

Special discounts on bulk quantities of Davies-Black books are available to corporations, professional associations, and other organizations. For details, contact the Director of Book Sales at Davies-Black Publishing, an imprint of Consulting Psychologists Press, Inc., 3803 East Bayshore Road, Palo Alto, CA 94303; 650-691-9123; fax 650-623-9271.

Davies-Black and colophon are registered trademarks of Consulting Psychologists Press, Inc.

Head & Shoulders is a registered trademark of Procter & Gamble.

Visit the Davies-Black Publishing website at www.daviesblack.com.

05 04 03 02 01   10 9 8 7 6 5 4 3 2 1

Printed in the United States of America

Library of Congress Cataloging-in-Publication Data

Williams, Caitlin
  Successful woman's guide to working smart : ten strengths that matter most / Caitlin Williams.—1st ed.
     p. cm.
  Includes bibliographical references (p.) and index.
  ISBN 0-89106-156-8 (pbk.)
  1. Success in business. 2. Businesswomen. 3. Women—Life skills guides.
  I. Title.

  HF5386 .W4995 2001
  650.1'082—dc21

2001028575

FIRST EDITION
First printing 2001

The book is dedicated to Tom,
who always knew,
and to Bud,
who always believed

Contents

Acknowledgments

THIS BOOK IS POSSIBLE because of the support, the words of wisdom, and the generosity of spirit of many fine people. First, my thanks go to Melinda Adams Merino, who first believed in this project and encouraged me to pursue it. Equal thanks go to Alan Shrader, my editor at Davies-Black, for his guidance, gentle good humor, and support in steering me through this project. Thanks also to Jill Anderson-Wilson for shepherding this book through its final stages and to everyone else at Davies-Black who helped make the book possible. And thanks to Mark Savickas, who first introduced me to the study of career development and to some of the ideas that helped me address the topic of balance in this volume.

Next, thanks for the support and helpful feedback from a number of great women who offered me their time and their thoughtful perspective including Joyce Prosser, Deb Humphreys, Brenna Hajek, Sandra Gustavson, Wendy Altmire, Vicky Adams, and Susan Nelson. These women helped me stay focused on the important issues that needed to be addressed and they offered a source of ongoing encouragement.

Thanks also for the ongoing support from Ansel and Nancy Woldt, Julie Brown, Michael Madison, David Humphreys, and Rose and Ray Thompson. An equal measure of thanks goes to Amy, Nate, and Charles Pluto for their willingness to help in so many unique ways. Thanks to Rose Mraz, whose words, actions, and life continually demonstrate what caring is all about. And last, but of course not least, thanks to my husband, Tom Mraz, whose faith, patience, and extraordinary culinary skills truly got me through. All these people remind me what a difference a close circle of friends, family, and caring colleagues can make. I feel honored to have them as a part of my life.

I also want to express my gratitude to the hundreds of women I've met, spoken to, and received letters from over the past five years. It was your comments, questions, and powerful stories that kept me pointed in the right direction. You taught me—and you continue to teach me—how strong and resilient women truly are.

About the Author

CAITLIN WILLIAMS holds a doctoral degree in counseling psychology with an emphasis on career development from Kent State University. For the past ten years, she has researched the factors that help women succeed in the workplace in healthy ways, and from her research she has developed a popular teaching model, *The Ten Strengths That Matter Most*. As president of Successful Working Women, Inc., in Westlake, Ohio, Williams offers workshops and presentations on this model, and she also speaks and writes on other topics related to women's workplace success.

Williams has worked extensively in designing and delivering career, professional, and personal development programs in business, industry, and education. She is also active in researching and speaking on cutting-edge trends and issues in the workplace and on Boomer lifestyle issues. She has written for business and career publications including *National Business Employment Weekly* and *Training & Development Magazine*, and online for the ASTD Career Page and PlanetKnowHow.com.

Williams is a member of Business and Professional Women, USA, American Association for University Women, World Future Society, American Society for Training & Development, Career Planning & Adult Development Network, Career Masters Institute, American Business Women's Association, National Speakers Association, and Women's-Vision Foundation. Her focus and passion is supporting women in their quest for meaningful work and healthy balance. When she's not speaking, writing, or teaching, Williams and her husband, Tom Mraz, spend as much time as possible exploring the Pacific Northwest.

Introduction

WOMEN ALREADY HAVE what it takes to succeed. We know that. So do the smart companies that hire and promote us. We've done our homework, gotten our degrees, paid our dues, and spent more than enough time in the pipeline. We've taken on team leadership roles, moved into management slots, and begun to join the ranks of senior executives. And at the same time, we're realistic enough to know that we still have our work cut out for us, as women have not yet reached parity in several industries and many organizations

So, where do we go from here? How do we best position ourselves at the beginning of the new millennium? Perhaps the first and most important item on working women's agenda in this brand-new century is the need to shift our strategy for moving toward success. Our challenge in the workplace of the past century was to push hard and find or make a place for ourselves—investing energy in earning our way into positions, proving we could do it, and struggling to fit in.

But, in the workplace of today and tomorrow, our major challenge has changed. With our experience, education, and growing record of achievement, we need to shift our focus to demonstrating our skills, contributing our talent, and taking our place at the table where the work gets shaped, the strategies get created, and the decisions get made.

It's not a matter of asking permission to be let in and accepted. Today's business environment, with its emphasis on speed, innovation, technology, and people skills, has changed the workplace dramatically. And it's in this new workplace that women's contributions become so important. Sally Helgesen, author of *Everyday Revolutionaries* (1998), said it quite well at a recent American Management Association conference (1999) for executive women:

> As women, we need to recognize and celebrate our strengths. What women have to bring to organizations is absolutely appropriate, indeed, essential for what organizations need to be able to succeed in this environment. . . . We are just what is needed.

It's women's ability to recognize our strengths and combine them with a solid understanding of what matters most to today's organizations that will lead to career success. That is what *Successful Woman's Guide to Working Smart* is all about. It's also about further developing and honing these strengths and finding ways to capitalize on them so that we and our organizations will succeed. This book offers key strategies for bringing your talents and skills to a workplace hungry for what you have to offer. It provides a new way to think about and create a career and a life that truly matter.

How This Book Came to Be

This book is based on more than twelve years of research, scores of individual and group interviews, dozens of workshops and career counseling sessions, and a thorough review of the best practices of successful working women and cutting-edge organizations. The result, *Successful Woman's Guide to Working Smart*, focuses on the core questions for working women at the beginning of the twenty-first century: What helps us succeed in today's workplace? What keeps us thriving and on the cutting edge?

I've heard repeatedly from working women that they need a focused, user-friendly, easily digestible resource that shows where they should be putting their attention to move toward their professional dreams. That's exactly what this book is.

Why This Book Is Important Now

Working women have come a tremendous distance over the past three decades and gained a clear awareness of what is needed to succeed in a business environment. Yet recent dramatic changes in the workplace, coupled with a growing understanding of women's unique strengths, make it vital for women today to approach their careers by seeing with new eyes. "Seeing with new eyes" means asking "Why not?" instead of "Why?" when it comes to the new and different. It also means paying attention to the following principles and determining how best to capitalize on them.

#1 SUCCESS HAS A MUCH BROADER DEFINITION THAN IT EVER DID BEFORE.
Never before have women had such an opportunity to fully explore how they want to shape their careers and their lives. Shaping a definition of success means taking the time to reflect on—and then clearly articulate and fully commit to a vision of—a career and a life that matter. Women who don't take the time to do such reflecting will falter, get distracted, or fail to see opportunities.

Successful Woman's Guide to Working Smart looks at current views of success and satisfaction and challenges you to examine your own. It also guides you toward a career that's based on a much larger picture of a successful, satisfying life and directs you toward realistic ways of moving in that direction.

#2 OUR WORKPLACE IS BEING REINVENTED EVERY DAY.
The workplace has been turned upside down, to put it mildly, and we're just beginning to feel the repercussions of this change. And along with the workplace itself changing, the whole notion of how, where, and when work gets done is up for discussion.

Whether we're ready or not, this new workplace will present us with one opportunity after another to try out new ways of shaping our lives and our careers. At times, these opportunities will feel exciting and energizing. At other times, we may find ourselves wishing for a return to the way things used to be—where the path was a bit clearer and where our actions generally produced consistent, familiar results. But the bottom line is this: The advantage will go to those who can make the most of all the new economy has to offer.

To position ourselves for these opportunities, it's critical for all women—those currently pursuing careers, those entering or reentering the workplace, and those considering a career transition—to understand today's new workplace rules. This book helps you understand and respond to today's changing workplace and develop strategies geared specifically to capitalizing on opportunities in the new world of work.

#3 "JOBS" ARE DEAD. TODAY'S FOCUS IS ON "DOING THE WORK THAT NEEDS DOING."

Advancing your career today means letting go of such old ideas as job descriptions and job duties. It means focusing instead on what's essential in the new workplace—what William Bridges (1994) describes as finding and doing "the work that needs doing" in our organizations.

This book will come back to the theme of "the work that needs doing" repeatedly because that's where the action is today. Women have always been flexible when it comes to trying out new possibilities; shifting the way we view our work represents one more opportunity for us to demonstrate that flexibility. Once we develop a new way to see the work that needs doing, we'll be ahead of the game when it comes to moving toward success. *Successful Woman's Guide to Working Smart* will point you in the right direction.

#4 SOME OLD ISSUES STILL NEED ATTENTION.

In spite of the significant progress women have made in the workplace, we still face some of the same issues that women before us faced. Many of us still struggle with trying to be both superwoman and supermom, leaving little time and energy for our own interests and needs. Our roles and responsibilities, and the expectations put on us, continue to become more complex, both in the workplace and in our personal lives. This holds true regardless of age, lifestyle considerations, or relationship commitments.

It's not just the work/family/life debate that's still with us, either. The glass ceiling and the sticky floor dilemmas continue to block women's access to positions with more power, influence, and opportunity. As a study done by the Society for Human Resource Management (1999) found, barriers still do exist.

That these challenges are still with us is testimony to how deeply rooted and pervasive they are and how important it is to consider new methods for counteracting them. *Successful Woman's Guide to Working Smart* examines these issues with fresh eyes and offers new approaches for dealing with these ongoing challenges. It provides an in-depth exploration of these complexities in the lives of working women of all ages and presents the latest information on how to enhance your quality of life, whatever your life circumstances.

#5 THERE ARE MORE OPPORTUNITIES THAN EVER— IF YOU KNOW WHERE AND HOW TO LOOK FOR THEM— AND HOW TO CAPITALIZE ON THEM ONCE YOU'VE FOUND THEM.

Opportunities for women have changed and grown significantly, even in the past decade. Right now, as you sit reading this book, new positions needing new skills are being created. The Women's Bureau at the Department of Labor (1992) notes that

> Between 1998 and 2008, U.S. employment will rise to 160.8 million from 140.5 million. This represents an increase of 14 percent, or 20.3 million jobs. Many of these new job opportunities will benefit persons seeking employment in computer and health-related occupations, social services, legal, natural science, teaching, and financial sales areas.

And according to a report from the Department of Labor's first National Working Women's Summit (1998),

> Our highly technological, increasingly competitive world economy requires— and rewards—workers with the best skills. Research conducted for the Women's Bureau has shown that jobs that have a computer component pay about 16 percent more than the same job without computer use. Between 1994 and 2005, computer-related employment will jump by an estimated 60 percent nationwide. . . . It is critical for women . . . to know what fields are promising, what kinds of skills are necessary to enter those fields, and where to find the education and training necessary to obtain those skills.

It's critical that women know how to find all possible opportunities for themselves. The Women's Bureau also reports that women's labor force growth is expected to increase at a faster rate than men's. And, as women's presence across occupations and industries becomes the norm rather than the token it used to be, women's opportunities will increase further. *Successful Woman's Guide to Working Smart* offers a forward-looking perspective on these opportunities and provides information on how best to capitalize on them.

#6 WE'RE GLOBAL, AND THAT MEANS WOMEN NEED TO THINK GLOBALLY—AND THINK OPPORTUNITIES.

Everyone living on this planet today knows that we're global. But just what do those two words "we're global" mean to you and to the way you go about living your life every day? Being global affects just about every aspect of our lives, from the movies we see and the music we hear, to the increased diversity of our neighborhoods and workplaces, to the way we shop and communicate. Day by day our lives get richer, more textured, and more complex through the contributions of many cultures and traditions.

What does being global mean for working women? Business journals and management texts today highlight the fact that women often bring strengths to the table that give them an edge in a global workplace. What once were called "soft skills"—those skills that enhance understanding and communication with others—are now a prized capability for doing business both inside and outside this country. *Successful Woman's Guide to Working Smart* looks closely at the highly valued skills and talents that women can offer and shows you how to practice global thinking as you go about shaping your own career.

Who Can Benefit from This Book

This book is for you, if you are

- A woman of any age who is entering or reentering the workforce, considering a change in your career or work setting, or wanting to succeed in work you already have
- A human resource professional who wants to recruit, develop, retain, and make full use of the talents of your female workers
- A career counselor or coach committed to helping your female clients shape a meaningful life for themselves

This book can be a valuable resource for you, if any of these scenarios describes your life or current concerns:

- You want a career *and* a life
- You love your work and want to grow even further in your chosen field

- You don't want to leave your job but don't want to just "show up" each day either
- You're good at what you do but can't seem to parlay your skills into something better

How This Book Is Organized

The four parts of *Successful Woman's Guide to Working Smart* cover the Four Themes of the the Ten Strengths That Matter Most—those key skills and attitudes that I've found through my research and interviews to be the most critical to career success for women in the workplace today. Within the four parts, each Strength is examined in an individual chapter.

Chapters 1 through 10 will take you on a step-by-step journey through all the Strengths, with ideas, examples, stories, and suggestions for weaving each Strength into your life. In each chapter, look for these special highlights:

Strength profile: A discussion of each Strength designed to give you an understanding of it and why it's important.

Portraits of strength: Examples of women who have faced a particular dilemma or challenge and used one of the Strengths to deal with that challenge and advance their careers.

Strength-building activities: Activities offering opportunities to reflect on how well you're capitalizing on each Strength right now and to try out new ways of thinking or acting to advance your career.

Making the most of each Strength: Practical ideas for putting each Strength to work for you right now.

Chapter 11 provides a user-friendly action plan that will give you a chance to take what you've learned and put it into practice. Consider it your own professional development plan.

How to Use This Book

This book asks you to take yourself seriously—and that includes taking your gifts, passions, and talents seriously. It means taking your efforts to build and shape a meaningful life for yourself seriously. It also means

The Ten Strengths That Matter Most

THEME 1: INNER RESILIENCE
Strength 1: Confidence
Strength 2: Self-Reliance
Strength 3: Planfulness and Initiative

THEME 2: CAREER ENHANCEMENT
Strength 4: Knowledge, Skills, and Learning
Strength 5: Interpersonal Competence
Strength 6: Flexibility and Savvy

THEME 3: QUALITY OF LIFE
Strength 7: Balance
Strength 8: Coping and Self-Care

THEME 4: THE BIG PICTURE
Strength 9: Awareness of Opportunities
Strength 10: Creativity and Leadership

asking questions of yourself, listening to the answers you get, and then honoring these answers through your actions and your choices. As women, we so often can "yes, but" or "not now" ourselves. We can be very convincing and talk ourselves into or out of just about anything. But if we take our answers and ourselves seriously, we can begin immediately to get closer to a life that matters.

This book also asks you to take yourself lightly. That means reflecting on your new learning without being harsh or judgmental of yourself. It also means "lightening up" by taking the opportunity to gain a different perspective on yourself, your life, and your possibilities. Try out some "what if" scenarios. Break out of any box you may have squeezed yourself into. Play with boldness.

Finally, turn each page with your mind and heart open to new possibilities for moving toward a life and a career that truly matter to you.

Overview and Survey

If a friend or colleague were to ask you the following questions, how would you respond?

Do you have a plan for advancing in your career?
Are you positioning yourself to take advantage of key opportunities?
Have you been making the connections you need to make?
Are you focusing on what's essential?
Have you figured out just how to keep up with it all?

These questions capture many of the top concerns I've heard from the women I work with, and chances are good that these questions touch on your concerns, as well. How would you like some help in answering these questions as well as others that reflect today's key career issues? Take the inventory that begins on page 10. It's a short questionnaire designed to help you identify both your greatest assets and those areas that could benefit from some attention—with a goal of moving you closer to a successful and satisfying career. Your answers to this inventory can give you the foundation for developing a clear strategy for advancing in your professional life.

Before you go any farther into the book, take twenty minutes or so to complete the inventory and then score it following the scoring guidelines. Answer as openly and accurately as you can. This inventory is for your eyes only, so use it and this book as tools to help you succeed in your professional life. Remember, this isn't a "test" where a high score means you're successful and a low score means you're not. Your score on this inventory is just a quick assessment aimed at giving you an idea about how well you're using the Ten Strengths That Matter Most in your career at the present time. After you've scored the inventory, turn to pages 17 and 18 for a description of the Four Themes and the Ten Strengths That Matter Most. Review your scores on the inventory using the list of Strengths to determine how well you're capitalizing on each Strength in your career right now.

Your scores on the inventory will give you a "snapshot" of where you stand across ten important dimensions of career success. The inventory can't predict the direction you're heading in, but it can help you focus your attention on key areas that will help you succeed in your career in the days ahead. The remainder of this book offers you strategies to address these key career areas and gives you suggestions for shaping your career in the future. By consistently practicing and capitalizing on these strategies, you'll significantly increase your chances for career success.

The Ten Strengths That Matter Most Inventory

DIRECTIONS

Consider where you are right now in your career and then assess yourself on the following statements. For each statement, check the box from 1 to 5 that best describes your belief or behavior at the present time, using the following guidelines.

5 – ALWAYS: You consistently, from day to day, are in agreement with the statement or perform the behavior described.

4 – OFTEN: You generally agree with the statement or perform the behavior at least once a week.

3 – SOMETIMES: You somewhat agree with the statement or perform the behavior at least once a month.

2 – SELDOM: You agree with the statement or perform the behavior very irregularly, or with no consistent pattern.

1 – NEVER: You disagree with the statement or never perform the behavior.

If you aren't employed right now, answer the questions as you think you would respond if you were working. If it's been some time since you were in the workplace, you may have to use your imagination. Still, you can probably make a good guess as to the way you'd be thinking or acting if you were working right now, so let that be your guide.

1A. I am confident in my ability to succeed in my career.
☐ **5** Always ☐ **4** Often ☐ **3** Sometimes ☐ **2** Seldom ☐ **1** Never

1B. I perform all my work tasks and professional responsibilities without any self-doubts about my abilities.
☐ **5** Always ☐ **4** Often ☐ **3** Sometimes ☐ **2** Seldom ☐ **1** Never

2A. I am in charge of my career.
☐ **5** Always ☐ **4** Often ☐ **3** Sometimes ☐ **2** Seldom ☐ **1** Never

2B. I make sure that everything I do in my work shapes my career so that it moves in the direction that I want.
☐ **5** Always ☐ **4** Often ☐ **3** Sometimes ☐ **2** Seldom ☐ **1** Never

3A. Knowing where I'm going in my career is essential.
☐ **5** Always ☐ **4** Often ☐ **3** Sometimes ☐ **2** Seldom ☐ **1** Never

3AA. Stepping forward to make things happen in my career is necessary.
☐ **5** Always ☐ **4** Often ☐ **3** Sometimes ☐ **2** Seldom ☐ **1** Never

3B. I have taken the time to formulate a clear picture of what I want to be doing and where I want to be going in my career.
☐ **5** Always ☐ **4** Often ☐ **3** Sometimes ☐ **2** Seldom ☐ **1** Never

3BB. I take specific actions that move me toward my career goals.
☐ **5** Always ☐ **4** Often ☐ **3** Sometimes ☐ **2** Seldom ☐ **1** Never

4A. Having cutting-edge knowledge and skills is important to me.
☐ **5** Always ☐ **4** Often ☐ **3** Sometimes ☐ **2** Seldom ☐ **1** Never

4B. I take part in whatever learning opportunities I can find that keep me ahead of the learning curve in my profession.
☐ **5** Always ☐ **4** Often ☐ **3** Sometimes ☐ **2** Seldom ☐ **1** Never

5A. I value relationship building.
☐ **5** Always ☐ **4** Often ☐ **3** Sometimes ☐ **2** Seldom ☐ **1** Never

5B. I build and nurture relationships with people throughout my organization and with clients, customers, and partners outside my organization as well.
☐ **5** Always ☐ **4** Often ☐ **3** Sometimes ☐ **2** Seldom ☐ **1** Never

6A. I see change as a great opportunity.
☐ **5** Always ☐ **4** Often ☐ **3** Sometimes ☐ **2** Seldom ☐ **1** Never

6AA. Understanding the unspoken rules of an organization is important.
☐ **5** Always ☐ **4** Often ☐ **3** Sometimes ☐ **2** Seldom ☐ **1** Never

6B. I easily adapt to new situations.
☐ **5** Always ☐ **4** Often ☐ **3** Sometimes ☐ **2** Seldom ☐ **1** Never

6BB. I use the unspoken rules of my organization to make things happen and get things done.
☐ **5** Always ☐ **4** Often ☐ **3** Sometimes ☐ **2** Seldom ☐ **1** Never

7A. I view balance in my life as desirable and possible.
☐ **5** Always ☐ **4** Often ☐ **3** Sometimes ☐ **2** Seldom ☐ **1** Never

7B. I pursue two or more activities/hobbies/interests, outside my work setting, that are separate and distinct from my professional role and responsibilities.
☐ **5** Always ☐ **4** Often ☐ **3** Sometimes ☐ **2** Seldom ☐ **1** Never

8A. I value the relationships I have outside my work setting.
☐ **5** Always ☐ **4** Often ☐ **3** Sometimes ☐ **2** Seldom ☐ **1** Never

8B. I connect with two or more friends/family members that I turn to for socializing and support.
☐ **5** Always ☐ **4** Often ☐ **3** Sometimes ☐ **2** Seldom ☐ **1** Never

9A. It is essential to be able to spot an opportunity and understand its potential value.

☐ **5** Always ☐ **4** Often ☐ **3** Sometimes ☐ **2** Seldom ☐ **1** Never

9B. I create opportunities for myself.

☐ **5** Always ☐ **4** Often ☐ **3** Sometimes ☐ **2** Seldom ☐ **1** Never

10A. I have the capabilities to be a strong, creative leader.

☐ **5** Always ☐ **4** Often ☐ **3** Sometimes ☐ **2** Seldom ☐ **1** Never

10B. I contribute my unique strengths, my creativity, and my leadership skills to help my organization and myself succeed.

☐ **5** Always ☐ **4** Often ☐ **3** Sometimes ☐ **2** Seldom ☐ **1** Never

SCORING

1. **In the chart on page 14, fill in the number of the box you checked** for each of the twenty-four statements on the line following the question number.

2. **For statements 3A, 3AA, 3B, 3BB, 6A, 6AA, 6B, and 6BB,** multiply the number you checked by .5 and write that number on the appropriate line. For instance, if you checked 1 for any of these statements, multiply 1 by .5 and record .5 on the appropriate line; if you checked 2 for any of these statements, multiply 2 by .5 and record 1 on the appropriate line, and so forth.

3. **Now add up the figures in each column** and put the total for each column in the space provided. You will end up with four separate column scores, each representing one Theme.

4. **Finally, add together the four Theme scores** you've just obtained to get your total inventory score.

5. **Record this score** in the space provided.

STRENGTHS

Confidence	1A ____	Knowledge, Skills,	4A ____	Balance	7A ____	Awareness of	9A ____
	1B ____	& Learning	4B ____		7B ____	Opportunities	9B ____
Self-Reliance	2A ____	Interpersonal	5A ____	Coping &	8A ____	Creativity &	10A ____
	2B ____	Competence	5B ____	Self-Care	8B ____	Leadership	10B ____
Planfulness	3A ____	Flexibility	6A ____				
& Initiative	3AA ____	& Savvy	6AA ____				
(× .5)	3B ____	(× .5)	6B ____				
	3BB ____		6BB ____				

Totals _____   _____   _____   _____

COLUMN SCORES

_____   _____   _____   _____

Theme 1:	**Theme 2:**	**Theme 3:**	**Theme 4:**
Inner	**Career**	**Quality**	**The Big**
Resilience	**Enhancement**	**of Life**	**Picture**

TOTAL INVENTORY SCORE _____

KEY

YOUR SCORES TELL YOU

- How well you're doing on individual Strengths overall and how well you're doing on your attitude (your A score for each Strength) and on your behavior (your B score on each Strength)
- How well you're doing right now in each Theme area (your four separate Theme scores)
- How well you're doing across all ten dimensions of the Ten Strengths That Matter Most (your total inventory score)

- **Your A score for each Strength** represents how much you believe in the value of that particular Strength.

  An **A** score of **4–5** means that you strongly believe in the value of that Strength at the present time.

  An **A** score of **3** means that you believe in the value of that Strength to some extent at the present time.

  An **A** score of **1–2** means that you do not believe in the value of that Strength at the present time.

- **Your B score for each Strength** represents your behavior on that Strength—how much you're actually using that particular Strength in your work each day.

  A **B** score of **4–5** means that you practice that Strength to a large extent at the present time.

  A **B** score of **3** means that you practice that Strength somewhat at the present time.

  A **B** score of **1–2** means that you're not practicing that Strength at the present time.

- **Your combined A and B scores** viewed together **represent your total individual score** for each Strength. This combined score represents how well you are able to fully capitalize on a particular Strength at the present time.

- **A total individual Strength score** (your **A and B score together** on a Strength) **of 8–10** means that you're doing well at using this Strength to your advantage at the present time.

- **A total individual Strength score of 4–7** means that you're using the Strength to some advantage, but not enough to get any real payback or benefit from it.

- **A total individual Strength score of 1–3** means that you're not capitalizing on that particular Strength at all.

YOUR THEME SCORES

Your total score for each Theme (your four separate column scores) tells you how well you're doing on making the most of that particular Theme.

- **For Theme 1 and Theme 2**

  A total Theme score of 24–30 means that you are doing well on capitalizing on that particular Theme at the present time.

  A total Theme score of 18–23 means that you are using that Theme to some extent at the present time, but not enough to really make it work to your advantage.

  A total Theme score of 17 or below means that you are missing out on the benefits that could come from using this Theme in your career at the present time.

- **For Theme 3 and Theme 4**

  A total Theme score of 16–20 means that you are doing well on capitalizing on that particular Theme at the present time.

  A total Theme score of 12–15 means that you are using that Theme to some extent at the present time, but not enough to really make it work to your advantage.

  A total Theme score of 11 or below means that you are missing out on the benefits that could come from using this Theme in your career at the present time.

YOUR TOTAL INVENTORY SCORE

A total inventory score of 80–100 means that you are doing a great job of capitalizing on the Ten Strengths That Matter Most right now. You should consider how you can continue to grow in your profession, position yourself for further advancement, make your mark in your field, and further enrich your personal life. Use the appropriate ideas and suggestions in this book to guide you.

A total inventory score of 60–79 means that you understand the value of and benefit somewhat from practicing the Ten Strengths That Matter Most. However, you could significantly increase your potential for career success and satisfaction by further refining your use of the Strengths. In particular, consider how you can move your midrange scores to a higher level. Use the appropriate suggestions and ideas in this book to guide you.

A total inventory score of 59 or below means that you don't understand the value of or aren't able to apply the Ten Strengths That Matter Most in your career at the present time. You may want to consider how you can take better care of yourself personally and professionally right now. Identify one or two Strengths in which you obtained lower individual Strength scores and design a plan in which you can increasingly incorporate these Strengths into your daily work routine. Use the suggestions and ideas in this book to guide you.

After you've taken and scored the inventory, I invite you to read the remainder of this book paying particular attention to the chapters that reflect your highest and lowest inventory scores. High scores represent areas of significant skill, so reading chapters that reflect those skills will help you learn even more ways to capitalize on them. Low scores represent opportunities for great growth and development, so reading chapters that reflect areas of your low scores will give you what you need to formulate your own plan for moving ahead in those areas.

The Ten Strengths That Matter Most

THEME 1

INNER RESILIENCE: Core Strengths that enable a woman to see herself as worthy of regard and capable of shaping her life in the way that she desires

Strength 1   *Confidence:* Feelings of self-esteem and belief in one's ability to succeed in job- and career-related tasks

Strength 2   *Self-Reliance:* Sense of inner direction and trust in oneself

Strength 3   *Planfulness and Initiative:* Developing an open-ended plan and taking action to move toward a desired future

The Ten Strengths That Matter Most (continued)

THEME 2

CAREER ENHANCEMENT: Career-building Strengths that enable a woman to flourish in her professional life

Strength 4   *Knowledge, Skills, and Learning:* Demonstrated expertise and a commitment to professional development

Strength 5   *Interpersonal Competence:* Ease in relating to others and the ability to nurture and maintain relationships over time

Strength 6   *Flexibility and Savvy:* Changeability with a practical understanding of the dynamics of an organization and the skill to effectively present and position oneself and one's work within it

THEME 3

QUALITY OF LIFE: Nurturing Strengths that enable a woman to thrive in all aspects of her life

Strength 7   *Balance:* The ability to lead one's life with attention to wholeness and harmony

Strength 8   *Coping and Self-Care:* The ability to use self-nurturing strategies at work and in one's personal life

THEME 4

THE BIG PICTURE: Capstone Strengths that enable a woman to position herself for future success

Strength 9   *Awareness of Opportunities:* Alertness to opportunities with the ability to capitalize on them

Strength 10   *Creativity and Leadership:* The ability to see oneself as a leader with the skills, talent, and insight to successfully move oneself and one's organization into the future

PART ONE

Building Your Inner Resilience

THINK OF A woman you know. It could be your best friend, or your daughter, or the new woman in your company. She's the one who has just finished college and gotten a job doing just what she wants to be doing. Now, think of another woman you probably recognize—that co-worker who always lands the plum assignments. She's the one who seems to have an uncanny knack for being in the right place at the right time with just the right skills and savvy and—most important—the right "I can do it!" attitude. And finally, think of a woman you really admire—the one you respect so much because of her perseverance and guts—that woman in the community famous for her passion for pursuing a cause.

Can you picture these three women? Most of us can. We all know women like them. And they all have something in common. All three really like themselves, trust themselves, and know what they want their lives to look like.

That's what Theme 1: Inner Resilience is all about. The three Strengths that make up this first Theme—Confidence, Self-Reliance, and Planfulness and Initiative—all reflect an essential foundation that every working woman must have if she's interested in building a healthy, successful career. Nothing less will do.

Think for a moment about those times in your professional life when things have gotten a bit stormy, chaotic, or uncertain. How did you handle yourself? Probably, you learned and gained from the situation. That's what women who have mastered Theme 1 are able to do. Because they have taken the time to really work on Inner Resilience, they make it through these tough times and keep right on going. How? When all else around them seems up for grabs, they trust themselves enough to reset their compass to point to their own true north once again. And when they do, they not only survive—they usually profit in some way from the experience.

I've worked with women who have honed the art of resilience, and their efforts show up in their ability to snag promotions, move to other parts of the globe to do exciting work, and generally thrive in their working lives—even when things don't go their way. I've also worked with women who have gone for promotions, become devastated when they didn't get them, and had a hard time recovering. The difference between the two groups of women? Those in the first group have the ability to reach into their core of Inner Resilience to help them get through—no matter what life throws at them. Women in the second group lack such a reserve.

If you already have a strong foundation of Inner Resilience, this section will give you several ideas for continuing to grow and flourish. If, like most of the women I work with, you want to build a stronger foundation in self-confidence, self-trust, direction, and personal courage, then this section will definitely help you do these things. I invite you to turn the page and begin to develop a solid base of Inner Resilience. It's the first step in getting your career going in a way that truly matters to you.

CHAPTER 1

Confidence Is at the Core

IF I WERE to ask you what one quality you believe is the most important for succeeding in your career, which would you choose?

This is the first question I ask women who participate in my workshops. Although they mention a variety of different qualities initially, the one that wins the top spot every time is Confidence. Simply put, your level of Confidence in yourself will make the biggest difference in just about every aspect of your career. Successful women report that, with Confidence, they are able to step forward, contribute their knowledge, demonstrate their talent, and shape a career that gives them satisfaction and recognition. They also report that when they're feeling less Confidence, they tend to hang back, doubt themselves, and miss out on opportunities to demonstrate their strengths and advance their careers.

In today's workplace, one of your keys to success is your ability to let others know who you are, what you have to offer, and how you can make a difference in their organization. Gone are the days of showing up, getting hired to do specific tasks, and then quietly going about your business. The most successful working women today are those who say, "Hire me, put me on your team, make me part of your project—I can do it!" In today's work environment, you can see pretty quickly why Confidence plays such a pivotal role. No matter how strong your skills or how good your credentials, unless you can confidently put yourself out there, those other achievements won't matter. Confidence is the starting point from which everything else gets set in motion.

As you read through this chapter, and as you learn about the other nine Strengths throughout this book, you'll see that career success in this new century is all about being comfortable with who you are and being able to demonstrate all that you can do. That's why you'll need Confidence every step of the way. Developing Confidence—that is, trusting and valuing yourself—lays the foundation for the other nine Strengths that are required for career success.

Remembering Your Past Successes

Twenty years ago, women's career-related Confidence concerns often centered on entering professional positions and showing that they were capable of "making it"—in sales, management, or marketing—any area that had been, up until that time, a "man's world." Today the issues are somewhat different. Most women working in organizations have already experienced some degree of professional success. The areas in which most Confidence questions arise today tend to be those associated with women taking on more visible assignments, reaching for new opportunities, transitioning to different careers, or accepting more senior leadership positions.

And it's when these questions come up that one important fact often gets lost. Every woman I've ever worked with has a sense of Confidence in some area of her life. The area itself may vary—it may be Confidence as a manager, a board member, a parent, a professional, a salesperson, an artist, a skier, or a volunteer, or it can be any combination of these areas. No matter what her age, educational background, or experience, every woman has some core of Confidence. What can happen, though, when a woman moves into a new assignment, a new organization, or a new role where the stakes are higher than before, is that she may forget that she already has this core of Confidence. Instead of remembering her previous successes, she will see her situation only from the perspective of someone new who lacks needed skills or experience. It's this forgetting about past successes—rather than any deep-seated issue of low self-esteem or mistrust of one's abilities—that can lead to a decline in Confidence. What does it take to turn this situation around, if it should happen to you?

First and foremost, remember who you are—a woman who has already succeeded in other areas of her life. Don't let temporary self-doubts or anxiety keep you from trying something new. And don't assume that the anxiety you're feeling in the moment will stay with you after you've gained some level of comfort with your new role and spent some time in your new assignment.

Second, recall what it has taken to gain Confidence in the past. Do you remember other times in your life when you've tried something new? Maybe it was learning a new software program, a new language, or a new technique in conflict resolution. Whatever it was, you probably struggled with it a bit at the beginning, learning new words, new ideas, or new behaviors. That's always the first step; it happens to all of us every time we risk learning something new. It's a natural part of the process. Remember, if you're learning and growing, you will always go through this "apprenticeship" period.

Third, set yourself up for success. Your Confidence increases when you

- Have faith and trust in yourself
- Get a feel for your work and gain a sense of mastery in it
- Have some evidence of your successes
- Receive support
- Hold appropriate expectations
- Maintain an accurate and continually evolving picture of yourself

Setting yourself up for success through the six points listed above means focusing on two equally important elements that contribute to Confidence:

- Feelings of self-esteem
- Beliefs about your competence

Together, they enable you to say, This is who I am and this is what I have to offer.

Increasing Your Self-Esteem

Self-esteem centers on your ability to value and approve of yourself in your career efforts. If you feel good about yourself professionally, chances are high you'll also feel good about your work and take pride in your accomplishments. If you were fortunate enough to grow up in an environment that encouraged and supported you, your self-esteem will probably reflect that and remain relatively high in most situations. If the environment you grew up in didn't encourage you to trust yourself and build on your strengths, you may occasionally experience feelings of low self-esteem and self-doubt that can interfere with your ability to count on yourself to do what you think is best in work-related situations.

Meet Rennie, a woman whose low self-esteem is diminishing her ability to confidently move forward in her career.

RENNIE WAS DOING it again—staring at the carpet as though her life depended on it. The project leader had asked if anyone had suggestions or ideas. Just like in the last three meetings, Rennie had an idea. And just like in the last three meetings, she had panicked at the thought of suggesting it to six other people. So, instead of making eye contact with the leader or anyone else, she had quickly shifted her focus to the floor. Twenty minutes after the meeting ended, Rennie was still berating herself and wondering how she'd ever get the chance to demonstrate her skills and get more challenging work. Why didn't she speak up? she asked herself each time. And her answer each time was the same: Maybe her ideas weren't so great after all. Maybe she wasn't so smart—maybe she wasn't ready for more challenging work. . . .

Rennie's experience isn't that unusual. Many women hit snags of low self-esteem occasionally—testimony to the fact that females in our culture continue to deal with this issue. Whatever the reasons for the low self-esteem some women experience, however, the bottom line remains the same: If you don't identify and work to shift those instances when you feel low self-esteem in your career, you'll probably encounter some roadblocks to career success, regardless of your other efforts.

Setting yourself up for success and increasing your self-esteem in your career begins with having faith in and trusting yourself. If you find yourself in situations where you feel like Rennie, the place to start is acknowledging what you do know and what you have achieved. Because the basis of self-esteem is valuing and approving of yourself, getting a handle on your accomplishments is an essential first step. It also reinforces your trust and faith in your abilities. Activity 1 will help you get started.

Accomplishment Survey

DIRECTIONS

1. Reflect on your personal and professional accomplishments thus far. These include any efforts you may have made toward goals that were important to you, such as enrolling in college, finding your first professional job, putting together a budget, finishing a difficult project, or getting appointed to a board. Record your accomplishments in the left-hand column below.

2. Reflect on what it took for you to achieve each accomplishment you listed. What skills, knowledge, and personality characteristics led to your accomplishments? These are your anchors. They can remind you that you've already set yourself on the path toward success. Record them in the right-hand column below.

Accomplishment	Skills, knowledge, personality characteristics
-----------------------------------	---
-----------------------------------	---
-----------------------------------	---
-----------------------------------	---
-----------------------------------	---

Since self-esteem rests on valuing and approving of yourself, getting a handle on your accomplishments as you've done in this exercise is an essential first step. It also reinforces your trust and faith in your abilities.

Believing in Your Ability

Your belief in your ability to succeed—to take the necessary actions in your job and in your career—is every bit as important as self-esteem. Judging yourself as capable (or not capable) is referred to as self-efficacy— it's your expectation about whether you can successfully perform a given behavior (Bandura, 1977). If you expect that you can do what it takes, you have high self-efficacy. Alternatively, if you don't expect that you can do what it takes to succeed at whatever it is you're about to attempt, then you have low self-efficacy. Possessing high self-efficacy is an important aspect of achieving success because it reflects your faith and trust in your own abilities.

As important as it is to have the appropriate training, experience, skills, and savvy to succeed in your career, if you don't see yourself as competent and capable of performing whatever behavior is called for, then no amount of knowledge or skill will matter. Your efforts at trying to succeed would be like pouring water into a container with a hole in it—you would always end up with an empty container.

Gail Hackett and Nancy Betz (1981) have looked extensively at the effects of self-efficacy on women's overall career development. They report that

> efficacy expectations determine whether or not a behavior will be initiated, how much effort will be expended, and how long the behavior will be sustained in the face of obstacles. (p. 328)

In other words, if a woman's self-efficacy is high—if she expects that she'll succeed at whatever it is she's about to do—it's more likely she'll try something new, really invest herself in the experience, and hang in there, even when the going gets tough.

Here's why Hackett and Betz's observations about self-efficacy are so relevant for those who want to succeed in today's workplace. Much of the work around us these days is project work—assignments that are often demanding and sometimes unpredictable. Such work requires initiative, persistence, and the ability to push through a project when support wavers or pressures increase. In this kind of work environment, self-efficacy becomes a required survival skill. When you're challenged with work that's new or that stretches you further than anything you've done before, your expectation that you'll succeed will help get you through. As the saying goes, if you expect you can, you can. If you expect you can't, you probably won't.

Although feelings of low self-efficacy can sabotage your career advancement, there are some things you can do about it. Worksheet 1 will show you some key areas to watch out for.

Determining Your Level of Self-Efficacy

DIRECTIONS

Read each statement and put a checkmark in the box that reflects your level of agreement.

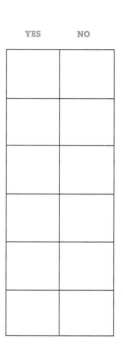

	YES	NO
1. Do you avoid programs or training that could "fast-track" you into a new career?		
2. Do you turn down promotions that could advance your career?		
3. Do you stay away from more visible assignments where others will evaluate your performance?		
4. Do you stay with the tried and true rather than take a risk and stretch yourself?		
5. Do you sign up for a class and then later drop out when you face some difficulties with the course?		
6. Do you initiate new projects and then consider giving up when you hit a snag?		

SCORING/INTERPRETATION

If you answered yes to any of the questions in the assessment, low self-efficacy may be getting in your way. Consider trying out the ideas that follow to help you turn your situation around.

- If you answered yes to question 1 or 2, your level of self-efficacy may be influencing your career-related choices. If it's low, it can keep you from choosing career opportunities that you're really interested in pursuing but avoid because you're concerned you might not succeed.

If you'd like to pursue a degree or sign up for some training, identify some women who have already been there and done that. Ask them how they managed to return to school or what helped them get through some particularly challenging training. When others who have already succeeded share their experience, it can ease your own anxiety and remove some of the unknowns in a new situation. If your company has a mentoring program, check out the possibility of getting some support through the help of a mentor.

- If you answered yes to question 3 or 4, your level of self-efficacy may be limiting how well you'll perform in your chosen career area.

If you find that you worry about how you might do in a situation where you're going to be evaluated and this worry is causing you to freeze up, consider working with a counselor, coach, or employee assistance program (EAP) representative. Also, pay attention to any negative self-talk you may be imposing on yourself. Are you increasing your anxiety level by criticizing yourself? Putting yourself down or telling yourself you can't do what you'd like to can't help but be an obstacle. If you are giving yourself any negative messages, you're sabotaging yourself. Talk this over with someone and figure out ways to short-circuit or replace these negative messages.

If you're concerned about how well you'll do at a new task, why not stack the cards in your favor? If you're considering returning to school for a degree, or if it's been a while since you've been back and you'd like to go for some graduate courses, why not participate in a class you know you'll enjoy and do well in? For instance, when you register for classes the first term back, sign up for one, not three! And make sure that one class is one you'll enjoy. If you've always liked math or tech-related subjects, sign up for one of those first. If you never enjoyed literature classes, don't go for one of those immediately. Get a couple successes under your belt before tackling something you believe may be more difficult.

- If you answered yes to question 5 or 6, your level of self-efficacy may be undermining your persistence in an area that could advance your career.

If you're concerned about being able to stay with something once you've started it, set yourself up for success. If the project seems overwhelming, divide it into manageable chunks. If you fear rejection, get some support to see it through.

Research has shown that a woman who believes in herself and trusts herself will continue in the face of adversity. If you can commit to staying with something that's difficult, whether it's a relationship, a tough project, or an unexpected challenge, you'll benefit in two ways: You'll have the satisfaction of seeing something through to completion and you'll increase your self-regard.

Getting to Know Yourself

If you're serious about pursuing a career and a life that matter, there's no better place to start than getting to know yourself. Intimate knowledge of your strengths and weaknesses is necessary for every step of your career journey, but it's most essential for Confidence. If you don't know what your strengths are, you surely won't be in a position to demonstrate them to others and you won't trust yourself to come through in circumstances where you really need to shine.

Under what circumstances do you notice your Confidence slipping? When do you feel that a low level of Confidence holds you back from something you'd like to pursue? Notice—even if it feels a bit uncomfortable to do so—the next time you feel unsure of yourself. Become more aware of what people or situations trigger any negative feelings. If you can identify when and how this process happens, you can more easily substitute healthy new behaviors and begin to reverse some of the old negative habits that get in your way. Activity 2 will help you recognize your Confidence strengths and weaknesses.

Confidence Inventory   ACTIVITY 2

DIRECTIONS

Read questions 1 through 4 and jot down some of your first thoughts. Put these questions aside and simply reflect on them for the next twenty-four hours. Then come back to the questions and answer them more completely. In answering these questions, pay particular attention to what you learned about yourself that you may not have realized before. Also, determine how you can address the areas you uncovered that could use some further attention.

Answer questions 5 through 9, paying attention to what it is about these interactions that makes you feel unsure of or good about yourself. Then determine how you can take better care of yourself the next time you're in a similar uncomfortable situation, or how you can increase the kinds of interactions that are enjoyable.

1. What is it that you really admire and appreciate about yourself?

2. What is the one thing you can always count on yourself for, no matter how difficult a situation might be?

3. What strengths do you have that others may not know about?

4. What are the ways you tend to sabotage your own success? What are the habits that keep you from moving forward?

5. Do you notice your Confidence slipping when you interact with certain people? Is there something about the way you're interacting with these people that is causing a problem, or is it the issue you're discussing that's causing you concern?

6. Who are the people and what are the circumstances that seem to bring out the best in you?

7. How do you handle new situations, such as the start-up of a new project or the first days on a new job? Do you begin things with a sense of anxiety and worry each time? If so, what is it that makes you feel uneasy?

8. What are the aspects of new situations that get you excited and ready to jump in? What aspects of new opportunities do you most enjoy?

9. How do you feel when you're in the limelight—when you're the point person on a team or the representative for your organization? Does it feel good to have opportunities to put yourself out there? Or do you worry about how well you're presenting yourself?

Checking Your Self-Expectations

At times, women place such high expectations on themselves that nothing less than perfection will do. If you tend to take this route, it's likely that you'll often feel less than confident in your work. Even though the "superwoman" days are supposedly behind us, there are still some women who continue to try to do it all—and do it perfectly. Especially in those situations you encounter for the first time, it's important to remember that anything new you attempt will increase your chances of making mistakes. That's the nature of growth, especially in the new workplace. And the more you grow, the more likely you are to make mistakes. But rather than label these moments as failures, consider reinterpreting them more realistically. Think of them instead as a series of approximations: Each attempt gets you closer to a sense of mastery and a feeling of Confidence.

If impossibly high standards continue to get in your way, chances are good you'll disappoint yourself over and over again. If you suspect that extremely high self-expectations might be an issue for you, get some input from others. You may be looking at yourself through too harsh a lens. Here are some helpful strategies.

SUGGESTIONS AND STRATEGIES

- Talk to women who know you well and whose opinions you trust. Share with them the expectations you have for yourself and ask for their take on your concern.

- Bring up with a group of women the subject of expectations. The sharing that comes out of such a group conversation may shed light on what many in the group are experiencing. It's amazing—when we hear the impossible expectations other women have for themselves, we can begin to look at our own expectations in a new light and then laugh about them together. Talking with others will give you the opportunity to do a reality check and begin to appreciate your work performance at its current level, rather than put yourself down for what you haven't been able to accomplish.

Developing a Portfolio

A portfolio is a way of documenting all that you've done. Keeping a portfolio of your accomplishments is a very useful tool that can continually reinforce your sense of Confidence. Beyond that, a portfolio is also a necessity in today's work environment, where reorganization and unexpected changes happen frequently. If you choose to make a career move, your portfolio will show your next employer what value you bring with you.

If you don't already have one, begin to put your portfolio together. To start with, your portfolio should include your work history, not just your accomplishments in your current organization. It should also include projects you've been involved in—both those that were wildly successful and those that didn't go as well as you would have liked. Chances are good you learned a lot in any project you worked on, so each of your efforts should be documented, along with the lessons you learned along the way. When it comes time to assemble a condensed version of your portfolio for showing to others, you can limit it to those projects that best highlight your work. But, for now, begin by including the whole range of projects you've been involved in.

Here are some things to include:

- Records of your education, any internships, cooperative work experiences, continuing professional development, and any special awards and certifications you've earned
- Past performance appraisals that detail competencies you've gained and goals you've reached
- Descriptions of the positions you've held, task forces you've served on, and committees you've been a part of or chaired
- Descriptions of team efforts that you have participated in, including your contribution to the team, along with what the team accomplished together
- Records of any professional activities you participate in, along with any special designations you've received
- Volunteer activities and community initiatives, such as literacy programs or school board involvement
- Descriptions of special assignments you've taken on, including the circumstances and what you contributed
- Records of international assignments and any special training or orientations you went through to prepare for these assignments
- Personal accomplishments that show motivation, perseverance, and creativity
- Records of technical training you've undertaken to update your skills
- Notes on any opportunities you've had to travel and live outside the United States, along with your level of fluency in other languages and your understanding of other cultures

Thinking about what you've accomplished and putting together evidence of your work can help you get a more accurate picture of your capabilities. To use your portfolio as a tool for increasing your Confidence, review it regularly and continue to add any new accomplishments throughout the year. Also consider the following suggestions.

- Take five minutes at the end of each day and reflect on what you accomplished that day.

- Buddy up with a friend and agree to share your successes with each other once a week. It's a great way to support each other and to begin to articulate your strengths and accomplishments.

- Review projects as you finish them and quiz yourself about what skills you gained that you didn't have before you took on the project. Jot down a list of these skills and keep your list with your other records of the project. On a regular basis, look these lists over, and make sure to add one for each new project.

Getting Career Encouragement

"ONE OF THE THINGS I got from my mom was my confidence. She never held back on encouraging me to do what I wanted. She's always been supportive."
—*Kathryn Crestani, laboratory manager, environmental services firm*

Ongoing support will almost always increase your level of Confidence. Who supports your career? Who are your strongest advocates? If you don't have a number of people who regularly support and encourage you, you're missing out on a great opportunity to increase your Confidence and advance your long-term career success.

Phyllis Tharenou has looked at the factors that influence women's managerial advancement (Tharenou, Latimer, and Conroy, 1994). What she found in her research was that women who received career encouragement were the ones who were successful and got the training and experience they needed to advance.

Ongoing career encouragement offers a touchstone for reminding you what you're capable of and for supporting your efforts to push past self-imposed limitations. The encouragement you get to pursue your personal and professional dreams will continue to move you closer to the life you want for yourself.

Think of the teacher, spouse, partner, parent, coach, supervisor, or colleague who reminded you of the bigger picture when you were doubting yourself—the one who convinced you that you had what it took to go for that promotion. Such people are your sources of career encouragement. In Strength 5, Interpersonal Competence, you'll find a number of strategies for increasing your professional support system and widening your base of vital career encouragement. Before working on your network, though, take the time to work through Activity 3 so you'll be better prepared to ask for exactly what you want and need from your network.

Sources of Career Encouragement   ACTIVITY 3

DIRECTIONS

Answer the following questions.

1. Who has offered you career encouragement in the past? How has it helped you? How have you grown as a result of it?

2. In your career right now, where and from whom could you look for support? (Check out company- or professional association–sponsored mentoring programs.)

3. What kind of career encouragement would be most useful to you right now? Specifically, what skills, information, advice, or support would help you in your career at this time?

When it comes to career encouragement, it doesn't matter whether you're a sales trainee, the vice president of a division, or a project manager. Across the board, career encouragement can boost your Confidence, reinforce your skills, and give you the courage to take the next step forward in your life. If you have a source for career encouragement, don't underestimate its value. Let the people who encourage and support you know that you appreciate their interest. If you don't have a reliable source of career encouragement, you aren't alone. Many women are in the same boat. But the ones who take themselves seriously find avenues for getting support and then ask for what they need.

Reassessing the Way You See Yourself Professionally

To increase your level of Confidence, you need to take a good look at the image you hold of yourself. If your image is one of a woman who is growing, developing, and learning, it will be a big plus. If that's not your picture of yourself, it's time to adjust your view.

When you stop and reflect on how you generally handle yourself in your professional role, do you feel satisfied? Or do you tend to think of a million things that "need fixing"? Though most women are beginning to celebrate their own style of professionalism, some still get stuck in a "fixing" mind-set. Maybe you've noticed this "I'm still not good enough" trait in some of the women you know. They are the ones who "yes, but" themselves constantly and who seem to find something negative to say in response to anything positive you note about them. It could be their clothes, their contribution to the team's effort, or the new account they just landed. Point out how well they did and you're likely to hear about all they did wrong on their way to that accomplishment.

Such self-put-downs tend to diminish a woman—in her own eyes, as well as in the eyes of others. Though you may not think that you put yourself down in such obvious ways, you may want to reflect on how much you dismiss yourself in smaller, less obvious ways.

KELLY HAS BEEN an instructional designer for about six years now. She's taken the time and made the effort to get an MBA, and she's known in her department for her skill in designing excellent training interventions. Yet she consistently minimizes her contributions. When complimented, she usually shrugs it off. In performance reviews, she fails to bring up her contributions to new programs. When other staffers come to her with questions, she helps them out but responds with "It's no big thing" when they thank her. The result? Those around Kelly, as well as Kelly herself, have stopped noticing what she contributes. When a slot opened recently for a regional training manager, Kelly definitely had the capability, but because she had underplayed her abilities for so long, those who made the hiring decision underestimated her skills and weren't even aware of all that she could contribute to the position. As a result, Kelly wasn't seen as a contender for the job.

Does Kelly's story sound at all familiar to you? If it does, you're not alone. Though their performance is top-notch, many women regularly slight themselves, often without even being aware that they're doing so. Each slight diminishes their overall image as a confident and qualified professional. Look over the statements in Worksheet 2 and see how many you agree with.

Acknowledging Yourself

DIRECTIONS

Read each statement and put a checkmark in the box that reflects your level of agreement.

	YES	NO
1. I have a good idea of what I do well in my work.		
2. I acknowledge the praise and compliments of others.		
3. I have a sense of pride in my accomplishments.		
4. I don't shrug off the thanks I get from others.		
5. I make my accomplishments known to others.		

SCORING/INTERPRETATION

- If you agreed with most of these statements, you probably have a positive view of yourself and your capabilities and are well on your way to capitalizing on Confidence.

- If you weren't sure how much you could agree with some of the statements, it's worth your time to focus on how you might be shooting yourself in the foot in this area. Why go to all the effort of doing an outstanding job and then deny yourself the recognition you deserve? The next time you're recognized for your skill or knowledge, take it in. Incorporate the recognition you receive into the image you have of yourself as a successful professional.

"**WITH SELF-CONFIDENCE,** you can channel your energy into pursuing your personal best."

—*Mari Santana, community organizer, spokesperson for Head & Shoulders®*
Success through Self-Confidence motivational campaign, www.saludos.com

Challenging Outdated Views of Yourself

Are you making your career decisions based on who you are today—or who you were yesterday? Some women hang on to a static view of themselves and don't update it to take into account new skills they've gained and experience they've accumulated over time. If you're making decisions about your capabilities based on the level of skills you had five years ago, or even two years ago, you're selling yourself short and sabotaging your own success.

Remember Rennie, the woman whose story appeared at the beginning of this chapter? Here's how she worked on changing the view she had of herself.

RENNIE CAME IN to talk with me about how often she doubted herself and put herself down for not moving ahead. She spoke about getting down on herself in those moments when she seemed to shrink back from opportunities. She described her fear that she didn't know enough and might sound foolish. Yet, when I asked her to tell me more about her position, her professional development, and the projects she'd been involved in over the past four years, Rennie surprised herself as she listed all that she had accomplished. She confided that when she first took on her job she was worried that she didn't have much experience, so she made it her business to learn as much as she could.

But it wasn't until she reflected on how much she had achieved and how much she had grown over the past couple of years that a light came on for her. She was still seeing herself as the new kid on the block with little to offer, even though that was clearly not the case any longer. Once she realized that, she was able to acknowledge her strengths and started gaining new respect for herself. She also started speaking up more in meetings and contributing valuable knowledge that helped her division set some new goals for the coming year.

Making the Most of Confidence

One of the best ways to add Confidence to your strategies for succeeding in your career is to have a plan to guide you in situations in which you may feel vulnerable, especially in those that might shake your Confidence. Whether these situations are related to interactions with others, to new challenges, or to expectations you have of yourself, here are some guidelines to make Confidence more of a strength that can work for you.

SUGGESTIONS AND STRATEGIES

- *Ground yourself.* When we're unsure of ourselves, we tend to miss the big picture and any cues that could help us handle the situation. To ground yourself, all you need to do is take a few deep breaths and calm yourself. Breathe, look around, notice the people in your surroundings. Get a sense of yourself and your body, whether you're sitting or standing, speaking or listening. Use your senses to anchor you.

- *Survey your situation.* Again, pay attention to cues around you. What's needed here? If people are asking for something from you, listen carefully to what they are saying. Don't rush yourself into responding. Take a few minutes to figure out what's needed: Knowledge? Certain skills? Action? Get clear on what the situation calls for and then you'll be able to respond appropriately.

- *Check your expectations of yourself.* Are you expecting too much of yourself? Self-doubts can spring up when we're expecting a perfect performance from ourselves. A vision of yourself as superwoman is not helpful.

- *Reflect for a moment on your history of past successes*—either in situations like this one or in any other situation in which you've accomplished something you're proud of. Remember the self-efficacy equation: If you think you can, you can.

- *Remind yourself of all that you bring to the table.* Focus on your unique skill set and how it can help you in this situation.

- *Act from a position of strength.* Silence your inner critic. Focus on what you're doing, not on how you're doing it. No matter what your response to a situation, doing it from a position of Confidence in yourself can make all the difference.

CHAPTER 2

Self-Reliance Lets You Take Charge

IF THERE IS one attitude that can point you toward success in your career today, Arlene Burns—who lists her title on her business card as "freelance adventurer"—captures the essence of it: Self-Reliance. She says, "I couldn't have manipulated the way life unfolded. . . . Instead of controlling the world, I have tried to find balance within the flow of events. Like running a river, [I'm] always looking for the smooth path through the rapids." Though the world that Burns hangs out in is likely to be one of mountaintops and white-water rapids, her words are an apt metaphor for what it takes to succeed inside most organizations today. Control is no longer the most appropriate response; relying on yourself and your resources to "find balance within the flow of events" definitely is.

Today's de-jobbed, you're-on-your-own, free-agent business environment offers every worker a number of challenges: Find a niche for yourself, make the most of any situation, add value, and be ready for just about anything. The women who succeed at these challenges are the ones who can find their own "smooth path through the rapids" of today's ever-changing workplace. How do they find that path? By relying on a sense of inner direction and by trusting themselves. Such an attitude is nothing new for most of the women I've met and worked with. They've all practiced Self-Reliance for as long as they can remember. The good news is: You probably have, too, though you may not have thought about it in these terms. And the even better news is: In the new workplace, women's strength in Self-Reliance gives them an edge in capitalizing on all the opportunities that weren't available in yesterday's work world.

Why is Self-Reliance so important in today's workplace? In today's workplace you are totally, 100 percent in charge of your own career direction. Self-Reliance will help you deal more effectively with new workplace realities, such as changing jobs, downsizings and mergers, evolving job descriptions, and the new contract between employer and employee, which I'll discuss more later.

Every woman living in our high-speed, nonstop society today faces unexpected news and unanticipated workplace shifts every day. And we all scramble, in our own way, to make sense of these changes and find the best way to respond to them. Some women hunker down even harder, determined to control their lives (which may work in the short term, but generally not much farther than that). There's another group (and many of us may fall into this category after a really frustrating day) who tend to throw up their hands, say it's hopeless, and cry out, "I have no control over anything in my life—what's the use!" And others seem to weather the storm, find a new niche, or remold their lives into new, more interesting shapes. It's this last group that's worth aspiring toward. Their members include the self-reliant women who see workplace changes as opportunities just waiting for them.

If you look more closely at these successful women, you'll notice that they're generally not the ones trying hard to find something to hang onto when things get a bit chaotic or unpredictable. It's more likely that they're the ones who count on things shifting and realize they can rely on their own resources to make the most of any situation. That's what Self-Reliance is all about. And that's the strength that's needed more than ever today.

Gauging Your Self-Reliance Quotient

So here's the big question—the one that will determine how potentially successful you'll be in the new economy: *Just how self-reliant are you?* Use Worksheet 3 to gauge your Self-Reliance quotient.

DIRECTIONS

Read each statement and circle the response that reflects
your level of agreement.

1. What's your first reaction to office rumors that hint that another round of changes is planned in your organization? Are you likely to say to yourself,
   a. OK, let's see how it goes and what's in it for me.
   b. I've been through this before, I'm sure I can handle it again.
   c. Time to get out my Plan B (or C, or D).
   d. I think I'll lose it if they change things around here one more time.
   e. How can they do this? It's not fair!
   f. I wish they'd get their act together. How can I be expected to get anything done if they keep making changes?

2. How did you handle the last unexpected event that came your way?
   a. It wasn't as bad as I thought it would be. In fact, it got me motivated to try some new things.
   b. I was actually pleased with how I handled things.
   c. It was the best thing that could have happened to me—I learned a lot about myself.
   d. Not well: I don't think I can face any more changes for at least the next six months.
   e. It took me quite a while to get over the shock.
   f. I found it hard to think about doing things differently for about a month.

3. How do you react when things around you seem "out of control"?
   a. It's almost a thrill for me when things get a bit upside down.
   b. I tend to focus on what I can influence.
   c. I prefer to see each new situation as a challenge.
   d. Where I work things are always out of control. I might as well get used to it; there's nothing I can do about it anyway.
   e. I complain to whoever will listen.
   f. I start looking for a new job where things won't keep changing so often.

4. What do you generally do when you're confronted with a new problem?
   a. I see it as a puzzle and start figuring out how I want to handle it.
   b. I play it out in my head, looking for different ways to tackle it.
   c. I don't see it so much as a problem; I see it as an opportunity to try out a new behavior or skill.
   d. I get frustrated because I already have more than enough on my plate.
   e. I get a bit anxious and search for someone who can walk me through it.
   f. As long as I don't have to figure it out by myself, I'm usually OK.

5. How would your friends describe your reaction to being marooned alone on a desert island for a week? Would they say,
   a. No problem for her—she'd probably rig up her own satellite dish somehow.
   b. She'd love it—it would just be one more adventure for her to jump into.
   c. She's actually pretty good at figuring things out for herself. I bet she'd do just fine.
   d. Without her cell phone and computer, she'd be lost.
   e. She'd probably be figuring out whom to blame.
   f. To say she'd freak out would be putting it mildly.

6. In what ways have you been resourceful over the past month—in either your professional or your personal life?

SCORING/INTERPRETATION

Look back over your responses. Though there are no right or wrong answers to any of these questions, you should be able to see a pattern of how you tend to approach your life.

- In questions 1 through 5, responses a, b, and c reflect a more self-reliant perspective, and responses d, e, and f reflect a less self-reliant view.

- On question 6, you can estimate your Self-Reliance tendencies by how easily you came up with an example or two to fill in the blanks.

- If you're self-reliant, your pattern should show an ease in counting on yourself and your resources to get you through. If you're not so self-reliant, your pattern probably shows some discomfort when things shift around and some concern about how you'll deal with your situation.

- If you came out on the self-reliant end of the continuum on the assessment, it's important to continue to nourish those qualities in yourself, maybe pushing yourself a bit to become even more self-reliant. If you came out on the other end, your best bet is to focus your attention on building a stronger base of Self-Reliance.

Wherever you came out on the assessment, one of the best ways to begin using Self-Reliance is to start looking at your workplace and your career in a whole new light. Here's how William Bridges explains it: "Today's workers need to forget jobs completely and look instead for work that needs doing—and then set themselves up as the best way to get that work done" (1994, p. ix). The key words here are "work that needs doing," and the responsibility is on you to find that work. Taking on that responsibility frees you to think bigger than your job description, bigger than your position, and even bigger than the professional title you may go by, whether it's accountant, programmer, engineer, or marketing director.

As long as you can identify work that needs doing—and position yourself to do it—you'll have work. Your work may not be under the same job title you've held for the past three years, it may not be in the same division, and it may not even be in the same organization—but you'll always be employable.

If you're like a lot of the women I work with, you may already be thinking and acting in a self-reliant way. It's just that you haven't consciously labeled your actions as "responding to new workplace realities." You may be more like Amy, a woman I worked with who has a tendency to take herself and her actions on her own behalf for granted.

AMY IS A sales rep in her early thirties; she's the mother of two small children and she attends weekend classes to finish her degree. Amy is also a veteran of two downsizings and one company merger. Recently she shared her career progress and her concerns about her company's future with a trusted friend and colleague. After Amy explained how she'd made each transition, her friend commented on how well Amy had weathered all the career changes she'd been through and how she'd made each change work for her.

Amy's initial response was "Like I really had a choice! I just did what anybody else would have done." But the point is that Amy didn't do what everybody else would have done. She made some good decisions, acted on them, and came out ahead. Yet she shrugged off her skills and downplayed her capabilities. Only when her friend pointed these strengths out did Amy start noticing how well she actually had handled these difficult situations.

Are you like Amy? Do you take your strengths for granted? If you do, you're missing out on acknowledging some important skills—skills that can make you even more self-reliant and resilient. It's vital that you recognize your abilities in this area. You can't take full advantage of Self-Reliance unless you recognize that you have it and regularly tap into it in a purposeful way.

Taking Responsibility for Your Career

"YOUR CAREER IS LITERALLY your business. You own it as sole proprietor. You have one employee: yourself. You are in competition with millions of similar businesses; millions of employees all over the world."

—Andrew Grove, President and CEO, Intel Corporation, in 13 Secrets They Don't Teach You in Business School

It may be old news to you that the employer-employee contract has shifted significantly. But do you really know the effect this change has on you personally and professionally? Are you shaping and directing your career based on this knowledge? Activity 4 will help you get clearer about whether you're going by the old rules or the new ones.

Self-Responsibility

DIRECTIONS

Answer the following questions.

1. What should your employer be doing to advance your career?

2. What should you be doing to move your career along in the direction you want it to go in your organization?

3. Who determines what skills you need, you or your employer?

4. Who should be finding ways for you to gain these skills, you or your employer?

5. What does your employer owe you? What do you owe your employer?

It may surprise you to find that you have expectations of your employer. That's not a bad thing, but it may cause you to be less than fully prepared to take care of yourself. When I did outplacement work in large organizations in the early '90s, I heard story after story about employees who felt betrayed by a company that had promised them lifetime employment and a straight shot up the career ladder. Belief in those old promises dies hard. Yet, for your own good, you need to replace those old expectations with an understanding of this new reality: In today's workplace you are, without a doubt, totally in charge of your career.

Being in charge means that you cannot count on your degree or your past work history to guarantee you work tomorrow; nor can you count on your supervisor, your manager, or even a mentor to keep you updated on opportunities. *You* are responsible for updating your skills. *You* are the one who must have a "heads-up" attitude when it comes to knowing the trends, the issues, and the competitors who shape your field and your position. Taking responsibility for your career is a day-in, day-out proposition that influences every career choice you make.

The upside of self-responsibility is that you are free to shape and direct your career the way you'd like. You aren't confined to one organization, one position, or even one field forever. With self-responsibility, you're in a much better position to call the shots.

Becoming a Free Agent

The response to this emphasis on self-responsibility is the phenomenon known as *free agency*. And it's not just confined to the realms of the self-employed. The term *free agent*, and all that it implies, seems to show up everywhere. Scan your local library shelves, business periodicals, or favorite magazines and you're likely to see titles such as these:

- *Creating You & Co.* (Bridges, 1997)
- "Be Your Own Boss" (Porter, Porter, and Bennett, 1999)
- *We're All Self-Employed* (Hakim, 1995)

These titles apply not just to freelancers, temps, and contract workers, but to everyone. If the contract of the past, which promised job security in exchange for some acceptable measure of performance, is dead—and it is—then it's critical to understand that you ultimately work for yourself. And as a self-employed person, you are ultimately responsible for your own success. If you can't develop a free agent mind-set even though you work inside an organization, you're probably not as self-reliant as you could be.

Though the free agent mind-set may seem odd or uncomfortable at first, the more you can cultivate it, the more you'll be in the driver's seat when it comes to advancing in your career. Here are some words of encouragement on this issue from *Ten Major Trends . . .* (1998):

> Growth in free agency will forever change the employer-employee relationship. Lifetime employment with a single company will give way to a new contract in which employers provide the resources for workers to grow professionally, and workers contribute their expertise for as long as the relationship is mutually satisfying. (p. 24)

Reframing Control as Personal Power

Control remains an important element of Self-Reliance. But it's not the old version, control *over*, that matters most today. Time spent trying to get control *over* or wrestle control *away from* wastes energy and saps creativity. A more useful focus is to reframe control as *inner* personal power, the kind of power that gives you the ability to shape your career and your life.

Personal power comes from an *internal locus of control*—a term used to describe the belief that *you* can shape your career and your life. For example, a woman with an internal locus of control is one who feels she can influence a job interview by the way she handles herself and responds to interview questions. Chances are good that if she feels this way, she'll interview favorably.

People who believe they are powerless to do much about what happens to them have an *external locus of control*—a term used to describe the belief that outside forces and others shape your career and your life. A woman with an external locus of control may walk into an interview feeling it's all a matter of luck whether she'll do well. Because she feels little power over her ability to influence the interview and the hiring decision, she probably will not interview quite as well as she could. Why not? Because believing that your good fortune, or the direction of your career, or even your own accomplishments is a matter of luck or the whim of some outside force means you'll feel little motivation to act on your own behalf.

Where do you place yourself on the locus of control continuum? How do you usually see your circumstances? Do the things that happen to you happen because of outside forces? Did you get that last plum assignment because of luck? Or the whim of your boss? Or did you get it because you influenced the decision or even caused it to happen? Successful women are the ones who firmly believe that they can influence the direction of their lives.

It's essential that you believe you can choose and shape the direction of your career and your life. Women who feel that their lives have largely been decided for them by their parents, by their spouse, or by increasing family obligations need to feel a sense of ownership about where their lives are going. Indeed, believing you can shape your destiny can make the difference between choosing a satisfying career, taking risks, challenging the status quo, and demonstrating unique strengths or leading a passive, diminished life. For these reasons, it's important to ask yourself some hard questions about your customary way of viewing your circumstances and your ability to shape them.

Having an internal locus of control means that you have an inner sense of direction, which is essential when it comes to making career decisions. Decisions about whether to stay with your company if it's likely to soon merge with another, or whether to take the lateral transfer that seems like a good move, or what to do when you reach those inevitable forks in the road are all best made with an inner sense of direction.

Inner direction gives us a center to orient and guide ourselves by, even when everything around us is changing. Do you have that deep center? Most successful women do: It is what gets them through all the shifts in their personal and professional lives. You probably have that deep sense of inner direction, too. Sometimes using it is simply a matter of getting more in touch with it. It's important that you take the time to connect with it because it can remind you of your inner strength and it can offer you one more source of Self-Reliance.

Another way to gain more personal power is to pay attention to the way you respond to the new challenges that greet you at work each day. Martin Seligman (1990), a psychologist who has done some powerful work on what he terms *learned optimism,* believes that the way we handle obstacles and adversities in our workplace makes all the difference. Are you someone who tries hard and goes the extra mile when the going gets rough? Or do you give in to the obstacle? True, you may have little or no control over your situation, but you can control how you choose to see the situation and how you want to deal with it. Seligman says the messages we give ourselves about our situation can have a profound effect on whether we take an optimistic stance and move forward or take a pessimistic stance and falter. For instance, Katherine just learned that she did not get the position she interviewed for in her company (which would have meant a promotion). Here are some of the ways she explained her adverse situation to herself.

WELL, IT LOOKS like I didn't get the promotion. I know I interviewed well. Perhaps they were looking for a different mix of skills or they wanted someone more familiar with the operations of that department. And that doesn't mean I won't get the next position I go after. Anyway, I'm doing a good job in the position I'm in now and I'm still learning a lot, so I'll just keep my eyes open for other opportunities as they come up.

Contrast Katherine's response with that of Danni. Danni just went through a similar interview process in another department and she, too, did not get the position she wanted. But notice the difference in how Danni explained her missed opportunity to herself.

WELL, I DIDN'T get the promotion. I probably really messed up in the interview and gave them all the wrong answers. It seems like I blow every chance I have to get ahead. I'll probably never get out of this department.

From looking at the messages the two women gave themselves, it seems pretty likely that Katherine will keep pushing forward but Danni may not. As Seligman explains, learned optimism is just that: learned. For women who want to get a better handle on workplace circumstances that sometimes seem out of their control, practicing *learned* optimism skills—including giving themselves positive, encouraging messages— is a great way to become more optimistic, and more self-reliant as well.

In the last couple of difficult situations you had to deal with, what messages did you give yourself? It's worth your time to discern your own patterns because a pattern that leans toward optimism will give you more motivation to trust yourself and move forward. If you tend to view many of the roadblocks you encounter with pessimism, then it's to your benefit to determine how you can begin practicing some learned optimism skills to shift your perspective and advance your career. As Seligman puts it, "How you handle adversity in the workplace tends to have much more impact on your career than how you handle the good stuff" (quoted in Row, 1998, p. 196).

Starting from a Position of Strength

Of all the advice available today, perhaps none is more important or more basic than this from Peter Drucker (1999), one of the most respected voices on management today: "Start from a position of strength." Do you know what your strengths are? Getting to know your strengths, as well as your weaknesses, gives you a great starting point on the road to Self-Reliance. Think about it. How can you rely on yourself in good times and in difficult ones if you don't know your own strengths? Would you rely on others if you didn't first have a pretty good sense of who they were, what they could do, and what they couldn't do so well? Probably not. So why wouldn't the same criteria that you use to judge how much you're willing to depend on someone else apply to you? Take a moment and reflect on the questions in Activity 5.

Your Strengths	ACTIVITY 5

DIRECTIONS

Answer the following questions.

1. What strengths do you admire in yourself?

2. How much do you rely on these strengths at the present time?

3. How did you handle the last difficult situation you found yourself in?

4. What did you do well in that situation?

5. What do you wish you could have done differently?

6. If you could do one thing that would let you rely on yourself more easily, what would that one thing be?

7. What resources would you need to help you make that shift?

Some women know their strengths intimately and have a lifelong trust in themselves. Others have developed self-trust as a result of going through some huge life or career challenge in which they learned an incredible amount about themselves. Most women, however, gain trust in themselves by consciously learning more about themselves and their strengths and by determining what they need to do to practice relying on themselves more. Over time, and with patience, their trust in themselves grows.

Taking stock of your personal strengths, weaknesses, resources, and limitations is time well spent, and it's one of the best ways to build your Self-Reliance reserve. You can begin by noticing all the ways you handle situations each day. Do this and you'll learn more about how well you take responsibility for your career and your life. In a work world that is guaranteed to surprise you when you're least expecting it, you can't afford *not* to start building up your own Self-Reliance reserves.

Another useful strategy for practicing Self-Reliance is to focus on an expanded view of yourself beyond your role as a worker. When we're too focused on work, we become unidimensional and lose sight of all we are and all we value outside our professional role. We also risk becoming far too reliant on our worker identity. It's never too smart to put all your eggs in the same basket. Here's how Ruth worked with this concern.

THE DESIRE FOR more self-reliance came for Ruth when she realized that her personal as well as her professional dreams needed attention. Ruth had been putting in a sixty-hour workweek for much longer than she had agreed to. And what began as a temporary situation had become a life centered solely on work with no time for other passions in her life. After a growing dissatisfaction kept nudging her, she finally realized she had turned over all the power for the direction of her career and terms of her work life to her employer. It wasn't that she didn't like her work. She did. But anxiety about losing her position if she spoke up, coupled with the hope of a new position in the company in the near future (which hadn't yet materialized), had gotten her stuck in a difficult situation. The result? Ruth became resentful, unhappy, unproductive, and increasingly dependent on her employer for her future.

Ruth finally realized that she didn't like the direction she was headed in, didn't want to devote most of her waking hours to her work, and didn't want to leave her job. After some brainstorming and coaching, Ruth came up with a number of alternatives for taking more responsibility for her career direction and becoming more self-reliant. She also came up with a number of different ways of getting her work done. She presented the alternatives to her employer and together they fashioned a new work arrangement for her. Today Ruth is working in a way that satisfies her. And the best part? She acknowledges the inner resources she used to make this change happen.

Seeking Support from Others

Practicing Self-Reliance does not mean dismissing the support of others, toughing it out alone, or assuming you're all you need to get wherever it is you want to go. On the contrary, capitalizing on Self-Reliance means trusting your own resources while also knowing when to reach out to others. Women who are underrepresented in their field or organization and women who are single heads of households often isolate themselves and carry Self-Reliance way beyond the point where it's useful. Some women in such circumstances say they have learned from experience that the only person they can truly count on is themselves. But this is a sure route to burnout.

Successful women know when practicing Self-Reliance is the most appropriate response and when seeking support is the direction they need to go. Ask yourself if you're too self-reliant—if you find it hard to lean on others occasionally. If that's the case, your overuse of Self-Reliance may be an obstacle for you rather than the strength it could be. Find a small group of friends and colleagues you're willing to trust and try some limited support seeking. See if you can build up a network that you can begin to rely on in times when you'd like and need some support. This takes time, though, so be patient with yourself as you shift to a better balance between Self-Reliance and support from others.

Making the Most of Self-Reliance

Here's a simple checklist to keep you moving in a healthy self-reliant direction. Look it over and highlight the suggestions that would be most useful to you. See how you can incorporate them into your daily work life.

- *Challenge your expectations* regarding what your organization "owes you" or "should be doing for you" on a regular basis. Scale back expectations that aren't in line with current workplace realities.

- *Commit to developing your career* daily.

- *Update your portfolio* (discussed in Strength 1) and résumé on a regular basis.

- *Learn one new thing each week* about your industry, your organization, and your profession.

- *Understand and respect the new workplace rules*—and make them work for you.

- *Scan your organization on a regular basis.* Pay close attention to which positions may soon be on the "endangered" list. If yours is one of them, have your Plan B or Plan C in place.

- *Beware of romanticizing* the "good old days."

- *Stretch* beyond your past limitations.

- *Don't put all your eggs in one basket.* Don't rely too heavily on your degree, the skills you had when you started your job, your job title, or your organization to get you ahead tomorrow.

- *Look for images of women you admire* who have come to rely on themselves. Let them remind you that women have the resources to be self-reliant.

CHAPTER **3**

Planfulness and Initiative Keep You Moving

"**HOW DO YOU** plan to spend your one wild and precious life?" asks American writer Mary Oliver. A question like this is the best place to begin if you're truly interested in shaping a meaningful career for yourself. Other questions—such as whether you should take this job or that one, or whether you should grab this promotion or hold out for another one, or whether you should relocate to that state or stay in this one—are also important. But those questions need to be asked *after* you've taken the time to identify what and how you want to contribute to the world and after you've developed an open-ended plan to move you in that direction. Your success and happiness in life rest on your ability to move toward a vision of what makes you happiest and toward those opportunities that let you make a difference in the world in a way that only you can. Your success and happiness also rest on your willingness to continually reshape your vision throughout your life, so that you are always moving toward dreams and goals that are relevant to the life you want to live and in line with current workplace realities.

Though having the latest data on salary ranges and knowing the hot jobs and hot companies that are hiring can help you make smart choices, just possessing such information isn't enough. It may give you some important facts, but it can't offer you wisdom on how to shape your own path. That wisdom comes from addressing core questions before beginning to sort through career possibilities. Planfulness is a tool to help you do just that.

Being Planful Versus Having a Plan

For women today, there are an infinite number of ways to forge a successful career. An interview with any female top executive will show you that. It's no longer a matter of planning a career on the basis of a limited number of options. The challenge for today's women is shaping a career path that is directed by their passions, goals, and unique life circumstances and finding numerous possibilities that let them demonstrate their strengths. The emphasis of this Strength is on *being planful,* which reflects an attitude and a process, rather than on simply *having a plan,* which suggests a one-time activity. Planfulness extends beyond traditional career planning—which for many people still suggests moving in a linear, logical fashion toward one specific career goal. It's not that traditional career planning isn't a useful strategy; it is. But it just isn't comprehensive enough to meet the challenges of the twenty-first century. The chart below shows some of the ways in which Planfulness differs from traditional career planning.

Traditional Career Planning	Planfulness
Primary focus is career via matching up skills with job title	*Primary focus is integrated/whole life and doing work that needs doing*
Is event focused	Is a lifelong, ongoing process
Relies on identifying job openings	Focuses on thinking beyond jobs
Follows a logical, linear progression toward a goal	Is based on having an open-ended plan
Emphasizes pursuing clear objectives	Emphasizes openness to choices that can lead to new experiences
Uses a rational decision-making process	Builds uncertainty into all decision making
Leaves little to chance	Combines elements of planning and chance
Does not value intuition	Honors intuition

Traditional career planning was based on the belief that you discovered what you were good at and matched your capabilities to a job description within one company, and that took care of things for a good long time—sometimes until you retired. It was also based on the notion that you set a goal for yourself, determined the steps you'd take to get there, started along your path, and, eventually, by keeping your goal firmly in focus, arrived at your destination. Actually, that "one career and one job for life" model made its debut back in 1895, as the country moved from an agricultural base to an industrial one—a good reason it's not appropriate for the twenty-first century!

It's understandable if your strategy reflects some traditional career planning habits, and there may be a number of reasons for it. Maybe you received career guidance in high school or college five, ten, or more years ago when such models of planning made more sense. Or perhaps you've been employed in the same organization for a number of years and you haven't felt the need to contemplate any change in your career planning strategy. Or you may be employed in an organization that still relies on an orderly process for moving up the career ladder (but beware—even the majority of *these* organizations are in a state of transition, or will be soon).

Which approach are you using to chart your career? Activity 6 will help you determine whether you're shaping your career based on an older model of traditional career planning or on a Planfulness model more in line with current workplace realities. Your responses on this activity will give you a good indication of how well you are using Planfulness now.

Planfulness ACTIVITY 6

DIRECTIONS

Answer the following questions.

1. How much of the way you plan your career right now is based on the traditional model of career planning?

2 What percentage of your total career development efforts is going into the pursuit of one job or occupational title?

Planning Around the Certainty of Uncertainty

The fact that many jobs that were in abundance five years ago are headed for obsolescence tomorrow is reason enough to shift the way you plan your career. But there are other issues as well—like the fact that so much is unpredictable today. Watts Wacker and Jim Taylor (1997) say it quite simply. They suggest that you "start planning around the certainty of uncertainty" (p. 246). Their remark reflects the reality for many women today, including Cecile.

CECILE HAS BEEN in the marketing division of her company for five years now. She's moved up a bit and gotten some more visible assignments, and she knows she wants the director of marketing slot in her company. There's absolutely nothing wrong with wanting that slot. In fact, wanting it shows that Cecile has ambition and is forward looking. But look at what happens to Cecile on her way to her goal. She sets her sights on the position and begins charting her course to get it. Three months later, the marketing division reorganizes and begins focusing on new products and new strategies. That's fine, Cecile tells herself. There is no reason she can't still snag that position. It just might take a bit longer. Then, three months down the road, her company gets acquired by another and, again, the division's priorities shift. That's OK, too, she tells herself—she knows that she can put up with just about anything because she really wants that position. But then Cecile starts noticing that the whole thrust of the division is nothing like it used to be. In fact, she can barely recognize it. Six months later, a new VP comes along and changes things once again, and he even suggests that the position of director is likely to be phased out. Cecile throws up her hands in frustration and says, "This doesn't even look like the company I signed on with!"

Cecile's example isn't at all unusual. In fact, it's standard fare in many of today's workplaces. Imagine your own frustration if you, like Cecile, had devoted all your time and energy to "following the rules" to progress up a career ladder that would lead to the one specific job you wanted—only to have it disappear. Your frustration would be the result of following the *old* rules in a *new* economy. Setting out on a clearly charted, straightforward plan of action that leads to one specific goal just doesn't do it anymore.

Even the old adage "If you keep on doing what you've always done, you'll always get what you always got" doesn't apply anymore. Today's truth is more like, "If you keep on doing what you've always done, it won't guarantee you anything but being left behind." Is such news unsettling? Maybe. Does it mean a constantly shifting range of new possibilities? You bet. All the more reason to consider Planfulness as a more relevant strategy. That's what successful women do.

Deciding What Place a Career Holds in Your Life

The first step in developing a Planfulness mind-set is to decide what place you want your career to occupy in your life. Until recently, there's been an unspoken belief in our culture that work and career should play a central role in a person's life. But today, women's perspectives on work and career run the gamut. Some consider their career to be a sacred calling and they devote their entire lives to pursuing work that they believe in fervently. Others see their work as purely transactional: an activity in which they exchange their time for money or other compensation.

But the majority of women see their career as occupying some point between these two extremes. Most enjoy their career and what they get from it. They just want to shape a career that works for them and lets them be true to who they are. Every woman's decision about where to position her career in her life will be unique. And where she positions it will very likely shift over her lifetime just as her other priorities will. What remains the same for all women is the need to examine the issue of what career means and what place they want it to hold.

How you decide to position your career needs to be based on thoughtful consideration of the life you want to live. This is as true for a woman choosing a senior-level position that will keep her busy sixty-plus hours a week as it is for a woman trying to balance her first professional position with part-time classes and the responsibility of caring for aging parents. To maximize your possibilities for a satisfying and successful career, it's imperative that you consider both the work and nonwork aspects of your life. That's why Planfulness begins with the larger view.

If you're a hiker, you know the value of getting above the tree line. As you make your way up a mountain that's covered with trees, you may see some great vistas here and there, but it's hard to get a true sense of all that surrounds you. However, when your path finally takes you high enough to get above the trees you've been hiking through, you see things from a whole new angle. You're able to look out and truly appreciate the beauty of the entire landscape. The bigger life questions are like that. They offer you a larger perspective from which to view your life's journey.

Lifestyle questions are equally important. Unless you know how you want to shape the nonwork aspects of your life, that part will simply end up being time you're not working rather than a truly rich and meaningful portion of your life. Take some time to reflect on the bigger life and lifestyle questions in Activity 7.

Life Questions   ACTIVITY **7**

DIRECTIONS

Answer the following questions.

1. What makes you happy?

2. What is most important to you? What calls to you?

3. What are your criteria for success?

4. Where do you want to position your career in your life? If you want it to be central to your life right now, how will that affect other parts of your life? If you want it to be more peripheral, how will that affect career opportunities that may open up later?

5. What kind of lifestyle do you want for yourself?

6. What kind of work style lets you give the attention you want to your lifestyle?

7. Will the career you are pursuing afford you the lifestyle you want?

8. What kind of work makes sense for you to pursue at the present time, given your life passions, your current personal and family commitments, and any other responsibilities you have taken on?

9. What other dimensions of your life, separate from your career, do you want to nurture right now?

Identifying Your Strengths Through Self-Assessment

Self-assessment gives you a realistic appraisal of your strengths, skills, and capabilities, as well as areas needing further development. This kind of self-knowledge is essential in making smart career choices and for determining plans for your ongoing career development. A well-done self-assessment will also position you well in interviews, during performance appraisals, and in selection processes when you choose to go for more visible and responsible assignments. You can't sell yourself very well if you don't even know your own product. Activity 8 offers some questions to get you started in self-assessment.

Self-Assessment ACTIVITY 8

DIRECTIONS

Answer the following questions.

1. What talents and skills do you now have?

2. What skills and knowledge do you want to develop?

3. How marketable are the skills you have?

4. How can you gain the skills and knowledge you don't have, but need?

5. What work can you pursue that would capitalize on what you have to offer?

6. In what ways do you want to express your unique talents in the world?

There's no shortcut to getting to know your strengths and your skills. The time you spend doing it will pay off over and over again. Remember, the key to getting the most out of any self-assessment is intention. If you go at it with a jaded "been there, done that" attitude, or without interest in learning more about yourself, you'll get very little that will be useful to you. But, if you approach it with openness and positive expectations, you'll be rewarded with some new insights into your strengths that can help position you to take advantage of new career opportunities.

Remember, too, that self-assessment isn't a one-time event. Just as situations change, so do people. We grow, gain new skills, pick up valuable knowledge and experience, and change our views as we interact with our world. What made sense at twenty may not make sense at thirty. What was once a good career fit may now feel like a pinching shoe. But that's as it should be. Imagine how diminished and stagnant our lives would be if we didn't grow, or if our dreams didn't change, or if we never saw things from new angles.

It's not enough to know your talents and skills. You must also know how your skills translate into something of value in today's workplace. Job titles are not what employers are focusing on; they're seeking knowledge and a skill set that adds value to their bottom line. If you know your skills, you'll know how to highlight specific ones to take advantage of different opportunities as they arise. For example, as a professional in marketing, you may find that your work makes use of certain of your skills. But, as you look to expand your current level of responsibility at your agency—or perhaps pursue work at another one—you may find that some of the skills you aren't using are ones you need to emphasize to get that new position. You will need to "rebundle" your skills to show how they apply.

Spend some time thinking about how you contribute to the work of your organization. No matter what position you're in, you have your own style of demonstrating your skills. You lead, collaborate, offer feedback, and strategize in a way that's unique to you. That way represents your own special "brand" that gives you your own advantage. If you know yourself well enough to know your brand, you'll be more likely to choose opportunities that highlight your uniqueness while you add value.

Developing a Personal Vision

Whatever your position, life stage, or lifestyle, a compelling vision of the future you want to move toward is a great companion. If you've been in on the process of developing a vision or writing a mission statement for your organization, you're probably well versed in the rationale and techniques involved.

Your personal vision evolves from answering the questions posed earlier in this chapter about who you are and what your life is about. Your answers can give you the clarity to develop a powerful vision for your life—one that will help you find and stay on your true path. Staying on your true path was never more important than right now when distractions, stresses, and overload can send you spinning. A vision can help you turn toward what says "yes" to you in your life and turn away from what is not in your best interests.

Your personal vision doesn't have to follow any specific formula or be stated in any particular way. What is important is that you take the time, after you've answered the questions posed earlier in this chapter, to ask yourself the three questions in Activity 9.

Your Personal Vision ACTIVITY 9

DIRECTIONS

Answer the following questions.

1. What is your vision of your best and brightest self?

2. What is the future you want to move toward?

3. What do you see yourself doing to make a difference in the world?

When you can answer these questions in a way that excites and pleases you, you'll find that Planfulness becomes easier. Your answers will guide you in making everyday decisions that are in your best interests and help you forge a career path. If you can answer these three questions, you'll know whether opportunities that come up are going to take you farther along your path or if they're really just detours or dead ends.

Identifying Work That Needs Doing

Planfulness requires that you take into account current workplace realities in deciding on the kind of career you want to pursue. If you're glued to a vision of a career or a job title that's no longer in demand, even the best of your skills won't get you very far.

Planfulness means thinking outside the box to explore a wider array of career possibilities. For instance, if you have a job like bank teller—a position that may soon be on the "endangered" list—it won't do much good for you to continue looking for work as a bank teller. Instead, you can begin looking for other ways to use your skills and other settings that offer "work that needs doing" and that make use of your skills. By doing so, chances are good you'll increase your employability.

Another way to think outside the box is to scan the environment and identify new positions that will be needed in the near future and then consider how you could apply your skills to move into those positions. Strength 9, Awareness of Opportunities, will guide you in identifying and making the most of these options.

Developing Goals in Times of Uncertainty

Almost every woman I know has had to make a shift in a goal she was pursuing. This is natural. We may set out with a goal clearly in mind but as we get closer to it, we see it from a different perspective and revise it a bit. Or, on our way to a goal, something surprising happens. Perhaps we get an unexpected advancement, or we benefit from being in the right place at the right time with just the right mix of skills, or we make personal or professional connections that change our career path significantly. Or the unexpected may come through some shift in our personal life, such as a relocation, an illness, or a change in an important relationship.

The unexpected event often shifts our goals and we find ourselves doing something a bit different from what we had anticipated. These occurrences aren't aberrations. These days they're just the facts of life. Smart goal setting today calls for identifying a number of short-term goals that move you along but also keep you open to possibilities. So rather than see surprises as a glitch in your pursuit of your goals, why not make room for them or even invite them in? Keep a vision of your best and brightest self in mind when the unexpected happens and ask yourself how you can use this opportunity and what you can learn from this situation that will help you get closer to your personal vision.

Career researchers Kathleen Mitchell, Al Levin, and John Krumboltz (1999) suggest a great way to view such unpredictability: through a perspective they call *planned happenstance*, which means going forward toward your goals with an open-ended plan. With such a plan as a guide, you can stop to notice opportunities along the way. You can let your curiosity lead you to explore a path or a career that excites you but isn't quite in line with what you thought you would be doing. Having a planned happenstance perspective may mean letting yourself take on a contract assignment simply for the sake of what you can learn from it. As a result of that assignment, you may decide that contract work fits your lifestyle right now and choose to seek more contract work rather than pursue a permanent, full-time job. Planned happenstance combines moving toward your goals with some built-in leeway to investigate interesting options along the way. The key is never losing sight of your larger goal: a vision of the life you want to move toward. As long as you hold true to that, you'll find that there are dozens of ways to get where you want to go.

Stepping Forward

Planfulness, as important as it is, isn't enough; it's only half the equation for success. The other half of the equation is Initiative: taking all you've learned about yourself, including your personal vision, your unique skill set, and your open-ended plans, and stepping forward to make them a reality.

Initiative is the complement to planfulness. Your possibilities may be limitless, but without action, they remain only idle daydreams. In today's workplace, you'll need more than great ideas and dreams; you'll need follow-through on these ideas. Successful women are the ones who turn daydreams and possibilities into actions that make a difference in their own career and in their company's bottom line. Think of Planfulness as designing the path and Initiative as taking it. In chapter 2, we looked at the importance of Strength 2, Self-Reliance, which stresses finding the "work that needs doing." Once you've identified that work, Initiative represents the next logical step to move you forward and position yourself to do that work.

Working women today are demonstrating initiative across every profession, position level, and industry—and their Initiative is paying off in senior-level positions, better compensation, more personal empowerment, and greater opportunities to do exciting work that makes a difference. The biggest challenge for women today when it comes to Initiative is choosing when, where, and how to step forward—not determining whether they can.

At first glance, Initiative seems pretty straightforward. After all, in today's fast-paced culture, the phrase "go for it" seems the only guideline you need. Yet using Initiative to advance your career requires more reflection and sophistication than simply propelling yourself forward. Capitalizing on Initiative means choosing to act strategically in ways that make a difference for your department, your organization, or your own career, as Joyce's story illustrates.

JOYCE IS A good example of someone who knows how, when, and where to practice Initiative. She conducts training workshops for a national telecommunications company. After learning all the training programs inside and out and teaching them to clients numerous times, she realized that some supplemental materials would make a big difference. Such materials would help the clients better use what they had learned. So, in her spare time, she put together some additional materials and created some imaginative color-coded charts that were a big hit with the groups she presented them to. The result? When new products are introduced and more training is needed, Joyce's clients always request that she be the one to conduct the additional training.

Like Joyce, successful working women notice something that needs doing, something that could be improved on, or something that could make a difference for the company or the customer. And then they go ahead and do it. In the process, they move closer to their vision of the career they want for themselves.

To capitalize on Initiative, you need to practice it in ways that move you along the career path you've envisioned for yourself. Knowing what career path you're interested in pursuing gives you a framework for practicing Initiative. It can guide you in choosing opportunities to step forward and take risks that can move you in the direction you want to be going. So you might consider what opportunities you could initiate that could precipitate more assignments and responsibilities in this area. Activity 10 will help you determine how you can practice Initiative strategically.

DIRECTIONS

Answer the following questions.

1. What developmental opportunities or training will give you some important new skills? What steps do you need to take to participate in them?

2. Given that today's emphasis is shifting more to performance, what steps can you take to continually improve your own?

3. What gets you excited about your field? Based on what excites you, what kind of activity can you initiate that will get you more known in your field?

4. Who are the one or two people that you want to learn from at work? How can you volunteer to help them in a way that might make their lives easier and ratchet up your own learning?

5. Is initiating a project a good way to be using your energy right now? If so, will you be able to follow through on this project once you've committed to it?

6. How can you offer what you know to others in your department so that you will all gain from your effort?

7. Is there something that would be easy for you to take on that would make you more of a team member here?

8. Is there a new direction that would really help the team grow that you're willing to suggest?

9. Who needs mentoring or coaching that you could support and encourage?

10. How will what you do make a difference?

11. How might what you do contribute to your department or to your organization's bottom line?

12. How are efforts to practice Initiative and risk taking viewed in your organization? Are people reluctant to step forward because they're often penalized for doing so? If that's the case, how can you still find ways to take risks that will help you grow but won't get you sidelined or ignored?

13. How can you get a better sense of the best way to take some risks? Which employees seem to put themselves out there and earn respect and recognition for doing so? What can you learn from them?

14. How can you raise your tolerance for risk taking so that you continue to show initiative more frequently and in more visible ways?

Practicing Initiative

Demonstrating Initiative can get you to some exciting new ways of working and doing business. It can also take you out on some unfamiliar limbs. Such a perspective can bring bigger losses as well as significant gains, and it's important to realize this before you take Initiative. Seek support for yourself, either by getting colleagues, co-workers, mentors, or sponsors sold on your ideas before you present them, or by enlisting your personal supporters who believe in you, no matter what the outcome. Here are some tips that may be helpful.

- *Stay open-minded.* Leave yourself open to opportunities to demonstrate Initiative and take risks that may not relate directly to your career path but may help position you to learn new skills or widen your network. Only you will know when these moments seem right; trust your instincts and your own good judgment to guide you.

  Remember that there are mini-opportunities to practice Initiative a dozen times a day. Going out of your way to introduce yourself to a new employee, offering to brief a team member who can't make a meeting, or teaming up with a co-worker from another division at the next golf outing can all be great ways to initiate and expand your possibilities a step further.

- *Ask for what you want.* Research has shown that women don't get tapped often enough for the training or developmental assignments that are so crucial to their keeping up with the latest information in their industry and advancing in their careers. Successful women realize this and don't wait to be asked if they'd like to participate. They do the asking. They make the case for their participation and position themselves for more opportunities. Ask yourself how good you are at asking for what you want—and how you could get better at it.

- *Think before you act.* There is wisdom in thinking before you act, and Initiative needs to be tempered with reflection. Before you step forward to volunteer for something or announce your commitment to a big project, stop and reflect on whether your decision will take you in the direction you want to be going. Also be sure to reflect on everything that's already going on in your life to be sure the timing is right for you.

- *Recognize the value of small steps.* A beautiful phrase in Greg Levoy's book *Callings* (1997) instructs us in how best to proceed when stretching our capacity to take Initiative. The author describes an acquaintance's definition of a "doable" risk as one that's "where you are, and one step" (p. 256). Look at the lives of most successful women and you'll see a series of small steps—small risks—along with occasional leaps forward.

  Practicing Initiative in your career is often a matter of taking several small steps—making incremental movements forward, and coupling these with occasional leaps. Why not set yourself up for success? Develop your own tailored plan for taking Initiative that's based on knowing where you want to be heading. Reflect on what behaviors and opportunities will point you in that direction. Then focus on several small steps to get the process started.

  As you grow comfortable with taking small steps, you'll gain the confidence to identify and take bigger ones. A plan like this will challenge you, but it won't overwhelm or intimidate you. Using such a strategy, you'll experience a lot of small successes along the way that will give you the courage to take bolder risks and demonstrate your Initiative in broader areas of your life.

- *Decide what's appropriate risk taking for you.* Practicing Initiative means accepting some level of risk taking, such as offering an alternative perspective at a meeting or stepping forward when you may not know what the outcome will be. That's why it's important to know what you're willing to risk.

  Risk is in the eye of the beholder. What's risky to me may not be risky to you. We each have our own barometer for gauging the chances we take—for determining what feels reasonable and what feels beyond our limits. If you want to succeed at Initiative, it's important to know your limits and to honor them. It's equally important to challenge self-imposed limits that you may have outgrown.

  In going about our daily lives, we all operate to some extent within our own comfort zone. Most of the time this is a good thing. When we act from a position within our comfort zone, we're usually pretty confident. We're in known territory and this lets us go about our business rather sure of ourselves. The occasional risks we take from within our comfort zone are ones we deem reasonable, so they don't usually get us too concerned.

  But practicing Initiative successfully often means stepping forward to try something that's beyond what's comfortable and safe. It could be taking on an assignment that makes you more visible than you've ever been before. Or it might be speaking up and suggesting a new procedure at the next staff meeting. Only you know where your own edge is when it comes to venturing out. The great thing about taking Initiative is that no matter where you are in your ability to take risks, you can always stretch just a bit beyond your own comfort zone and, in doing so, continue to grow.

  If you're clear about your reasons for taking a risk and you're willing to push the envelope a bit, you'll probably learn a lot from the experience. Regardless of the outcome, chances are good you'll gain more confidence in your abilities and you'll begin to develop your own risk-taking style.

- *Break some rules.* Have you seen the television commercial with the tag line encouraging you to "color outside the lines"? Or the one that shows a weary executive at the end of a long hot summer day shedding his suit jacket and briefcase to run through a water sprinkler?

What do they have in common? Breaking the rules. Doing it differently than expected. These commercials are just mirroring a much larger unspoken belief that's part of every cutting-edge business today, which is: If the old rules no longer make sense, get rid of them. Cultivate nonconformity or, in the words of Wacker and Taylor in *The 500 Year Delta* (1997), "practice intelligent disobedience."

How do you do that? By constructively questioning the way it's "always been done" in your organization. By asking questions like Why not? What if? How else could we do this that might give us a better solution? What unique perspective can I offer that no one else can? Push out-of-the-box thinking one step further: Get rid of the box altogether and then see what you can create.

Making the Most of Planfulness and Initiative

Planfulness is a habit. As such, it can be started anytime, any day. It can be started now. Think of it as a backdrop from which you make life choices. One of the best ways to capitalize on Planfulness is to take the time to ask yourself the questions posed in this chapter. You don't need to go off on a ten-day retreat in Bali to answer these questions. Your backyard, a woodland path, or a quiet corner and a cup of tea will work just fine. And it doesn't matter what stage of life you're at. Your life is precious and important at every stage, from infancy through elderhood. And remember, too, that you'll have different answers to your questions at different life stages and in different life circumstances. That's why it's so important to do a self-assessment and examine these questions on an ongoing basis.

Practicing Initiative means taking actions—or not taking them— based on whether they bring you closer to wholeness in your life. When so much urges you forward, when things are going just right, and when opportunities seem to show up at every turn, you may still need to get a bigger picture of how your life is shaping up. Why? Because this is precisely the time when you are likely to forget what you said you wanted your life to be about. When you're a star, when you're exercising Initiative to the best of your ability, chances are you will be noticed and directed in career-enhancing ways. Getting a bigger picture can give you perspective on how well your career and your life are working. Reflecting on the bigger picture can help you decide whether it's a time to take on one more project or turn down a career-enhancing opportunity to have more time for another area of your life.

PART TWO

Developing Your Abilities to Enhance Your Career

THE STRENGTHS YOU'VE gained by building your Inner Resilience have laid a strong foundation for you to grow professionally and position yourself for success in your career. The Strengths that make up Theme 2: Career Enhancement—Knowledge, Skills, and Learning; Interpersonal Competence; and Flexibility and Savvy—all focus on the attitudes and actions that matter most in today's workplace.

To thrive in the world of work you must know what's most important in your profession. You have to understand what your organization values. You need to see multiple perspectives. And you must know how to build strong relationships if you want to accomplish anything of value.

Today's workplace is jam-packed full of possibilities, but there's no clearly documented set of directions for taking advantage of them. Maybe at some point in the past when things moved more slowly and events occurred more predictably, you knew which path offered advancement and success; but that's not the case today. Unless you know how to add value based on your brainpower, your people skills, and your ability to make things happen in your organization, you might as well pack up and go home, because those new possibilities won't be open to you.

Continuing to enhance your professional skills and acumen has never been more important. Theme 2 offers you a picture of the important issues inside today's workplace and gives you ideas for really making a difference there. If you can make a difference in your organization, chances are good you'll make a difference in your own career satisfaction and success as well.

CHAPTER 4

Knowledge, Skills, and Learning Make You Valuable

HERE ARE A few facts and figures that should get your attention:

- The World Wide Web grows by seventeen pages every second.
- Knowledge doubles about every seven years.
- Half of what students learn in their first year of college is obsolete by the time they graduate.
- By the second decade of this century, the amount of information available to us will be 10,000 times what's available to us today.
- "Must be able to learn at warp speed" is a new requirement for many job openings posted on the Internet.

Given statistics and expectations like these, what's your challenge as a working woman in the Information Society? To succeed in our new economy, you'll need to

- Know what's essential to keep yourself and your organization ahead
- Be smart about keeping up with new developments
- Show your organization that you possess the knowledge and skills to help it make a profit
- Nurture your capacity for ongoing learning

Strength 4 focuses on three critical interrelated components: Knowledge, Skills, and Learning. Your ability to use all three is essential if you want to contribute to your company's bottom line. If you can't do that, you can't help your company compete. Simply put, capitalizing on Knowledge, Skills, and Learning is key to your success in today's workplace.

But to do this, you'll need to forget the old K–12 (kindergarten through 12th grade) education model. Success today means embracing the new K–80+ (kindergarten through age eighty-plus) model of lifelong learning instead. Learning never stops. We all realize that the password in today's workplace is Knowledge. No longer are a successful company's most important assets found in its buildings, its equipment, or its other holdings; rather, they are found in its workforce: the holders of the Knowledge and Skills that keep the company competitive. The Knowledge, Skills, and Learning that you bring with you to work each day—what's referred to as human capital—are the key to your organization's success. They're the keys to your success as well.

Your ability to stay committed to your own growth and development—your own cutting edge—through continuous Learning will make you stand out and ensure your employability. Should your company downsize, you can simply take your very portable assets (your expertise) with you down the street, across the country, or halfway around the globe—to whoever is looking for what you have to offer.

Because today's knowledge-based workplace shifts the base of power from the organization to the individual, it offers you limitless opportunities. You can significantly leverage your career options if you focus on the essentials that follow.

Understanding What Knowledge and Skills Are Worth Having

"**THE JOBS THAT ARE** growing most rapidly in number also generally pay the best. These jobs require increasingly high levels of skill and knowledge."
—*Workforce 2020*

In my career development and job search classes I take the participants on a time-travel tour to give them the "long view" of the work that has needed doing—along with a picture of the Knowledge and Skills that were necessary to get that work done—from the hunter-gatherer societies, through the agrarian societies and into the industrial age, all the way to today's age of knowledge. It's easy to see that the work that has needed doing in the world has undergone numerous shifts over time, and each shift has dictated what specific Knowledge and Skills are valued. As a result of these shifts, the Knowledge and Skills that were vital yesterday may not be so important today or tomorrow.

Have your Knowledge and Skills evolved so that you're positioned to meet the demands that these shifts dictate? Are you able to do the work that most needs doing in your organization today? Are you regularly thinking about what work will need doing tomorrow, and what Knowledge and Skills it will require of you? Or are you still trying to solve today's workplace problems with yesterday's tools? The Skills we learned five, ten, or twenty years ago just don't have the value they once did. That's why it's so critical for women to update their Skills and Knowledge base continually.

Although this constant updating of Knowledge and Skills may seem a bit overwhelming, the good news is that organizations today fully understand that you can't possibly walk through their door knowing all there is to know. No one can. That's why training and development efforts inside organizations are gaining renewed attention. Your employer expects to upgrade, update, train, and cross-train you after you're hired. But you still have to show up with some expertise you can build on and an attitude that shows you can—and want to—learn.

Turning Information into Usable Knowledge

Figuring out how to identify, access, and capitalize on the most relevant information today can seem like a formidable task, and if you feel a bit breathless trying to keep up with the sheer volume of material available, you aren't alone. Complaints of "data overload" and "information fatigue syndrome" are on the rise. But there are some ways you can capture just the information you need to keep yourself and your organization on the cutting edge.

One way to make the most of all the bits and bytes that are floating around out there is to practice the art of making sense of the information you take in. Here's how. First, convert information you scan into Knowledge you can use. Next, apply that Knowledge to a project you're working on right now or consider how it could be used in a project that's coming up.

Here's how Carrie, an analyst in a marketing firm, used this converting and applying process to help her in her work.

LAST NIGHT, CARRIE picked up a magazine and began reading an article that included demographics on people who had recently relocated to the Southwest. For this article to be useful to her, it's not enough for Carrie to know just the figures reported in the article. She needs to be able to scan those figures and pull from them something that can help her in her work, noting, for example, how many people who have relocated are between the ages of fifty and sixty, a group that's been the focus of much of her recent research and work .

Carrie can also make the information in the article more useful by adding it to other boomer generation trends she's been tracking. She can put this information to work by incorporating it into the design of a marketing campaign she's creating for a client who's trying to sell his services to baby boomers.

Another way to make meaning out of all the information that crosses your desk and computer screen each day is to ask the "So what?" questions in Activity 11.

"So What?" — ACTIVITY **11**

DIRECTIONS

Pick out a story in today's newspaper and apply the following questions.

1. What does this information mean to you personally? (In other words, how could it affect your life?)

2. What does this information mean for your field or for your profession?

3. What does this information mean for your organization? For your organization's position globally?

By putting information to the "So what?" test, you can screen out a lot of useless bits and pieces, and, at the same time, you can screen in those trends, events, and news stories that can help you stay abreast of information pertinent to your field and your career. Try this technique the next time you decide to tackle the stack of reading material that's been accumulating on your nightstand.

In order to stay on your learning edge, you need to know what is important in your field. Look over the questions in Activity 12. If you can answer these questions, you already have a heads-up on what's important to you, your career, and your organization.

Assessing Your Learning Edge   ACTIVITY **12**

DIRECTIONS

Answer the following questions.

1. When was the last time you brought yourself up to speed in your field? (Hint: If it's been longer than six months, you're due for a tune-up.)

2. What are the latest trends, the cutting-edge research, and the newest applications in your area of expertise?

3. How much do you know about the direction your company is heading?

4. How well versed are you in the latest services and products in your line of work?

5. What are your competitors doing that your company isn't?

Using Self-Assessment for Feedback

Wherever you are in your career, you already possess a significant amount of Knowledge and Skills. If you've just recently finished formal schooling, you have a good handle on some of the latest trends and issues in your field. If you've been working, you have a history of valuable work experience and probably a good understanding of what's worth knowing in your company and your field—and what isn't.

Armed with the assets you already have, you certainly don't need to start from scratch to bring yourself up to speed and stand out as a star when it comes to this Strength. But it's critical to know where you stand in your profession and in your organization.

Self-assessment is essential when it comes to getting important feedback about how well you are practicing this Strength. You may be under the impression that you know just about all there is to know in your position or your profession. And that may be the case. But how did you reach that conclusion? How do you know you're as up-to-date in your area of expertise as you could be?

The specific technique you use for self-assessment is less important than your commitment to doing it. If you need some guidance in choosing a way to begin, here are some suggestions.

SUGGESTIONS AND STRATEGIES

- Focus on the skills assessment section of a career book such as the classic *What Color Is Your Parachute?* by Richard Bolles (be sure to get the latest edition).

- Try a skills card-sort activity such as the ones put out by Career Research and Testing in San Jose, California. Card sorts are an easy way to get a good snapshot of your current marketable Skills. Ask the career development resource person in your organization or the career counselor at your college about card sorts. He or she probably will have access to them or will be able to direct you where to go.

- Visit your local library and look for books related to skills assessment.

- Consider seeking the services of a career counselor or coach who can help you identify your Skills.

Understanding your Skills through assessment gives you a baseline. It confirms what your strengths are and provides useful information about areas of potential weakness. You can use this information—especially if you combine it with benchmarking, which is discussed next—to determine whether you are as up-to-date in your area as you need to be. You can also use it to consider opportunities to capitalize on your strengths in ways you may not be doing right now.

"**THE KEY DIVISION OF** the future is going to be between those with skills and those without, and will be defined less and less by gender."
—*Helen Wilkinson, author and feminist, Fast Company, December 1999*

Personal Benchmarking

Personal benchmarking gives you an edge by testing the worth of your Skills in the work world. It involves comparing your skill set with those of others doing similar work in your field to determine if your level of performance is about the same as theirs or if it's ahead of—or behind—the curve. Here are some strategies to get you going.

SUGGESTIONS AND STRATEGIES

- Look over journals, magazines, and websites that cover your profession. See what "best practices" they're discussing—what tools, techniques, and strategies others in your field are using to do their work.

- Attend at least one monthly meeting of an association you belong to (if you don't belong to any, consider joining one now). Listen to the issues and pay attention to the topics they're presenting.

- Attend a regional or national conference that covers your profession or area of current work. It's a great way to find out the latest trends, hear about organizations that are engaged in cutting-edge workplace practices, and network. You'll come away with a much better picture of how well your current Knowledge and Skills stack up against those of others in your field.

- If you can't attend a national or regional conference, see if you can get audiotapes of keynote presentations and breakout sessions covering cutting-edge topics.

- Make a coffee date with a colleague you admire and ask her what she's been reading lately. What issues does she think are important to pay attention to? What kinds of projects is she involved in?

- In getting together with others, be sure to include co-workers or colleagues from inside your organization who are doing similar work and also someone from outside your organization. That way you'll get an idea of how well your organization is keeping pace with others in the industry.

Consider whom you want to benchmark yourself against. If you compare yourself with others with a midlevel range of Skills and Knowledge, you'll get a general idea of what's current common practice.

In addition to comparing your Skills with those of colleagues at your level of experience and expertise, consider talking with someone who has not been around as long as you have but who has an insatiable desire to learn and make her mark in the field. Chances are good she knows the latest "big thing" on the horizon. Be sure to make this kind of benchmarking activity a reciprocal one; while you're asking about what she's paying attention to, figure out what you can offer that will take her a step farther in her journey as well.

Also consider benchmarking yourself against the leaders in your profession. If you do, you'll get a better idea of what Skills are on the cutting edge and what trends are just starting to surface. But prepare yourself: Comparing yourself with people who are pioneering in your field may leave you feeling you're behind where you should be. That's not necessarily the case, though; the people you've identified as leaders are stars who have made it their business to keep ahead of the rest. Learn from them, but don't set yourself up with unrealistic expectations.

In using any of these benchmarking strategies, ask yourself how well your Knowledge and Skills compare with what you're reading and with what you're hearing from all these different sources. Once you've done some benchmarking, identify one area you can focus on right now. Choose an area that you already have some interest in and want to learn more about. Then use one or more of these strategies to get up to speed.

SUGGESTIONS AND STRATEGIES

- Contact your professional association for a listing of their continuing education courses on audio- or videotape that would take your Knowledge or Skills to the next level.

- Check your local library for audio, video, or printed resources that would bring you up to speed in your chosen area. Make sure the resources you choose are current.

- Visit some virtual learning websites. You can probably find an offering for just about any topic you can imagine.

- Invite two or three women colleagues—from either inside or outside your organization—to get together on a regular basis, maybe once or twice a month. The purpose of your get-togethers is small-group "briefings" in which each person gives a ten-minute summary of a new book she's reading, or a technique or idea she's learned since the last get-together. You could also use the time to swap information about useful websites or seminars that are coming up.

- Commit to reading weekly one newspaper or one online business, technology, or career column that would teach you more about a topic you think is important to your success or to the success of your organization.

- At the next conference you attend, choose a breakout session that combines a presentation of cutting-edge information with a "hands-on" component so you can experiment and try out some of your new learnings.

- Listen to the headhunter the next time she calls, even if you're not looking for another position. Aside from it being politically wise to keep such relationships alive, you can learn a lot from hearing what kinds of Skills other organizations want in the people they hire.

Performance appraisals and 360-degree feedback can also be helpful in providing you with information on your Knowledge and Skills base. If your organization uses these tools, consider how they can help you kick your expertise up to the next level. It's important, however, to determine how valuable these resources really are for you. If your performance appraisals have been positive experiences that have accurately pointed out your strengths as well as the areas that need further development, that's great. But, if the appraisals and feedback you've received have been unduly negative or offered no opportunity for further learning, then they probably won't be useful to you here. These tools will take you farther only if they can help you move to your next level of expertise. Use only the tools that best help you get there.

Viewing Learning as an Attitude and an Activity

Learning is both an attitude and an activity. As an attitude, Learning is the way you approach opportunities that have the potential to teach you something new. Attitude can make the difference between whether you walk away from an opportunity smarter and more energized or simply a few hours older. One of the problems we face today is that we're inundated with so much stimulation that we begin to get glassy-eyed and tune out when we're presented with yet one more person, idea, or situation. But, if attending staff meetings, association dinners, and seminar sessions is how we've chosen to spend our time, do we really want to tune out for such a large portion of our waking hours? Why not walk into these events with our eyes and ears open to new opportunities? Learning requires attentiveness and a curiosity about taking in something new.

KATHLEEN VIEWS LEARNING as her chief way of approaching life, and she lets others know it. During her last job interview, Kathleen made sure the interviewer knew the Learning projects she was pursuing, and she emphasized her ability to be a "quick-learn" in new situations. Her points impressed the interviewer and helped her land the job.

As an activity, Learning involves taking advantage of an ever-growing list of options for gaining Knowledge and Skills, including formal Learning through classes or online venues that leads to a degree or certification, as well as training sponsored by an organization or profession. It also includes informal Learning opportunities such as conversations with colleagues, mentors, and coaches; stretch assignments; and travels to new destinations on business.

Pursuing Formal Education

"**I WAS ALWAYS TAUGHT** that education was my ticket to freedom. . . . It is something no one can take from you. It is something you will have your whole life."
—*Patricia Beller, Aquarist and Scientific Liaison between U.S. and Mexico,*
Stephen Birch Aquarium Museum, La Jolla, California, www.saludos.com

If you've determined that formal education would be valuable in bringing you up to speed on the Knowledge you need or that it would increase your opportunities in your organization, there are probably more ways to attain it than you imagine. Whether for a certificate or an undergraduate or graduate degree, innovative new programs are springing up everywhere to make it more convenient for you to get the education you need, even if your work schedule and your nonwork commitments are restrictive. Your library and the World Wide Web have information on these programs.

But pursuing an education still presents challenges, no matter how convenient the delivery options. You need to consider what kind of degree or program of study will work best for you. What is of greatest value in your profession? What kind of education is most marketable? What is it that your organization values? Try to answer these questions before signing on with any program. Your commitment to your education is going to take time and energy, no matter how convenient and worthwhile it is. Getting clear on why you're doing it and what you hope to get out of it will help you stay centered and motivated, especially when class papers, work assignments, and your six-year-old's homework all need your attention at the same time.

Just as it's important to ask questions in a job interview, it's equally important to ask questions when considering your education. Learn as much as you can about the program before you commit. Here are some questions to get you started when you talk to an admissions representative.

If it's a traditional program,

- What resources are available for you in the way of library materials, career counseling, financial aid, and academic advisors?
- How available are the professors?
- Does the program offer internships or a placement service (if these elements are important to you)?
- Can you talk to alumnae who have been through the program?
- Is it possible to sit in on a class?
- Will the program give you what you need and want?
- What's the institution's reputation in the community?
- Does the institution offer credit for prior Learning?

If the program is primarily an online Learning arrangement, it's important to ask,

- How do you enroll?
- What do your fees cover?
- What student services are available?
- How easy is it to get the class materials you'll need?
- How available are your professors?
- How are grades and records of your classes handled?
- Is this program part of an accredited institution's offerings?
- Whom can you talk with that's currently enrolled?
- How easily can you transfer your credits to other institutions?

Regardless of the kind of program you choose, if you have kids, a partner, or a spouse, talk with them about your decision to continue your education, and decide before classes begin how to share household obligations. If you live alone, let your friends know what kind of support and encouragement would be helpful. Get to know other students; they can be a great source of support. If there were ever a time to hang up your superwoman cape, the day you go back to school is the time to do it. You will be pressed for time, and you will increase your commitments. That doesn't mean you shouldn't try to do it all. It means you should consider how best to go about it.

One more critical area needs to be addressed. The American Association of University Women (1999) found that women, more than men, determine that they can't pursue schooling because of debt, children, age, or anxiety. If you are one of these women, don't come to the conclusion that you can't afford it or you can't manage it. If you think that, you won't succeed. Instead, get information and support to deal with your concerns and consider these facts as well.

- Women with a college degree can increase their earnings by as much as 75 percent over what they would earn with a high school diploma.
- Your salary over time affects your pension and social security benefits. Lower wages initially mean lower income later in life.
- College degrees and other types of advanced training and education multiply your choices of career paths. Lack of further education limits your career choices to positions that may be dead-ends or short on opportunities.

Some women automatically assume there's no money available to them. But that's not always the case. Talk with your manager or HR representative and find out what the tuition reimbursement policy is in your organization. Check with the financial aid office at the institution you're considering. Check with the women's groups you belong to; they may have scholarships available. Ask women you know, who have gone back to school, how they did it. And don't forget to check online as well. Some women's foundations set aside funds for women who want to pursue an education later in life, or for those who want to pursue a nontraditional career. Don't give up and say it isn't possible. Your future depends on it.

Does your organization have a corporate university? More and more organizations are offering their own full-blown educational programming. If you're not sure just how extensive your organization's offerings are, find out now. Promotions and advancements are sometimes tied to your participation in such programs. And it's just plain silly not to take advantage of these opportunities. Find out what's offered on your company's intranet, investigate what learning consortiums your company may be part of, and ask about what alliances it may have with educational institutions in your community. The better informed you are, the better able you'll be to put together your own ongoing Learning program.

When it comes to training, how often do you get it? And what kind of training is it that you're getting? Research by Tharenou, Latimer, and Conroy (1994) shows that participation in training often leads to managerial advancement, and the right training positions you for organizational opportunities. You can't expect to be a contender for high-level opportunities if you don't have the training—the Knowledge and Skills—that the position demands. Training also gives you visibility. Make it a point to learn about and participate in the best training that's available in your organization.

Seeking Developmental Assignments

Want a chance to learn, improve your Knowledge and Skills, and demonstrate your value? Assignments within your organization that give you a chance to try out what you know and challenge you to push yourself in novel situations can do just that. Do you know what opportunities are opening up that will give you a chance to improve or learn critical Skills? Have you identified areas in your company that you could transfer to that would push you to try out new capabilities? Are there people you'd like to be mentored by or special short-term projects you'd like to be a part of? Most successful women list a stretch assignment or participation in a visible project as part of what helped them succeed.

Don't expect these opportunities to come knocking on your door. Generally, they don't. You often need to take the Initiative. This is especially true when it comes to opportunities such as international assignments. Research indicates that incorrect assumptions and faulty generalizations about women not wanting to—or not being able to—take on such assignments keep many women from getting them. If you're interested in an international assignment, speak up and let those in charge of making such decisions know what you want.

There's also a new spin on global assignments that you may want to look into. Some organizations, realizing how much an assignment outside the country can disrupt an employee's life, have found ways to make such experiences possible via technology. Recent reports indicate that companies are offering overseas assignments to workers who never have to physically leave their home base. Global networking is making "virtual transfers" a new possibility.

Practicing Real-Time Reflection

With employers demanding that we learn at warp speed, we're faced with the challenge of figuring out just how to do this. When our schedules include back-to-back meetings, frequent travel, and tight deadlines, how and when can we reflect on what we're learning along the way? The notion of reflection—the ability to sift through our experiences and use them to direct our future plans and actions—is critical, yet the idea of practicing reflection can seem like an ivory-tower luxury in our lightning-fast workplace. But there is a way to use reflection as a valuable tool: It's called real-time reflection and it's worth your effort to try it out.

Chances are good that, in the course of your career, you've spent some time in "debriefing" after you've completed a Learning experience. You've stopped, reflected on the experience, and pondered how you could use whatever it is you learned—sort of a looking back and then looking forward process. In addition to these techniques, Kent Siebert (1996), who has studied executives' ability to learn from their experiences, found that consciously making efforts to learn *throughout* the time that we're involved in an experience can give us an edge. To maximize Learning and make it much more useful in the real world, Siebert recommends "inbriefing"—reflecting on what you're learning as you're doing it. Basically, Siebert suggests that we train ourselves to ask good questions while we're in the midst of an experience in order to get the greatest Learning from it. The next time you are in the midst of an experience— or even when you are transitioning from one activity to another— practice real-time reflection by asking yourself the questions in Activity 13.

Real-Time Reflection   ACTIVITY **13**

DIRECTIONS

Answer the following questions.

1. How can you focus on key issues and learning opportunities as you go through this experience?

2. How can you build opportunities to practice real-time reflection into the time you have available right now?

3. What are you learning that can be applied across all the dimensions of your work, and how will this Knowledge affect your co-workers and yourself?

Get into the habit of asking yourself Learning-focused questions throughout your workday. Your Knowledge and Skills base will likely increase, you'll make more connections between the work you're doing and that of the organization as a whole, and you'll be able to apply what you learn across a broader spectrum of work activities.

Creating a Professional Development Plan

Organizations today are invested in knowing and leveraging the value of their human capital—their workers' Knowledge, Skills, education, and experience. You should be just as invested in knowing and increasing the value of yours. Use the self-assessment and personal benchmarking strategies mentioned earlier in this chapter to determine your baseline. Then, using this information, create a Professional Development Plan for yourself.

Commit to this plan as seriously as you do other important projects you are responsible for. First, determine what specific Knowledge, Skills, and expertise you want to develop. Next, determine the resources you need and how you'll go about getting them. Consider both longer- and shorter-range activities. For instance, if you choose to go back to school, that goal may take a while to reach. Build in some shorter-term Learning goals as well, like attending a meeting of your association or scanning a publication once a month to look for new trends in your field. Regardless of your level of expertise right now, a good Professional Development Plan will move you ahead.

A Professional Development Plan is a commitment to your growth. It can be as detailed as a listing of the specific Skills and competencies you want to acquire and the way you'll go about acquiring them. Or it can be as broad as identifying areas you know need your attention based on some personal benchmarking you've done. The plan that will work best for you is one that takes into account both the Knowledge and Skills you want to pursue and your understanding of the ways you learn best.

As you implement your Professional Development Plan, you'll need focus. Focus will keep you on track when you need to decide among several Learning or development opportunities. It will remind you of what you're there for at the next conference you attend. Focus will help you accept one voluntary commitment over another in your professional association, based on which fits better into your plan. In addition to focus, it's also important to keep your plan open. It shouldn't be so rigid as to keep you from trying out an unexpected new opportunity. Your Professional Development Plan is part of your life, after all. It shouldn't be an onerous drag on your energies. It should be something initiated by you to keep you curious and pushing on your cutting edge.

Special Issues Related to Women

Everything in this chapter has pointed to the critical role that Knowledge, Skills, and Learning play in career success today. Reports indicate that this Strength is particularly important to women, and participation in activities related to increasing one's Skills and Knowledge has been shown to increase future career prospects. Yet, in the face of these facts, research continues to show that women are not getting the training and the developmental assignments they need to position themselves for managerial roles and success. Use the ideas presented throughout this chapter to make sure you're not missing out on important learning opportunities.

Making the Most of Knowledge, Skills, and Learning

Practicing this Strength does not require ten hours a day. It does require focus, a commitment to growth, and a hunger for learning that never stops. Here's some great advice from *Management Review* writer Tom Brown (1996), based on his interview with career development guru Douglas T. Hall.

> Learn how to learn from everyday work challenges. You're in a career development class every day . . . many of the challenges now facing you can teach you to stretch, think, and act in new ways. Master these "new lessons" and you have built a wider base of career competencies. The more you can develop yourself, the stronger you will be in the sense of being employable, if not immediately employed. It's employability that will provide security in the future. (p. 25)

Keeping these words in mind, try the suggestions on page 92.

- Find out as much as you can about the training and other learning opportunities in your organization. If you're new to an organization, it pays to learn about them and get placed in them early on.

- Talk to other women at your level in the organization and to senior-level women as well. Find out what programs they've participated in. Learn which programs are superior, and avoid the ones that shunt women off to the side. Determine what's critical to advancement in areas you're interested in and then take every opportunity you can to make a case for your participation. Point out the benefit to the organization if you participate.

- Learn where the stretch assignments are. Which assignments are fast-track opportunities? Talk to women who have gotten them and find out how you can position yourself for one.

- Do not wait for such assignments to show up at your cubicle. Use the Strengths of Initiative and Interpersonal Competence, discussed in other chapters of this book, to help you move toward them.

CHAPTER 5

Interpersonal Competence Is a Woman's Edge

IN AN INTERVIEW I did for a *National Business Employment Weekly* article highlighting the cutting-edge skills needed in a global workplace, I asked Jennifer Jarratt, vice president of Coates and Jarratt, a futurist firm that helps organizations stay ahead, "In our high-tech, computerized, faster-is-better workplace, what skills are among the most important for a worker to have?"

Jarratt's answer took me by surprise at first—until I stopped to reflect on it for a moment: the ability to play well with others. Ours is an age in which we can "reach out and touch someone" halfway around the globe but we can't quite connect with our co-worker one cubicle away. Proof of our need to do a better job at communicating is showing up everywhere.

- Business periodicals are reporting on the need for interpersonal skills across every imaginable industry, profession, and job title.
- Technical professionals are being urged to move beyond "computerese" to better relate to their nontechnical co-workers.
- Incidences of worker isolation and rudeness are on the upswing.

- A recent survey ("Listen Up," 1999) found that 80 percent of executives polled rated listening as the most important skill in the workplace today—and 28 percent rated it as the one most lacking!

Advances in technology have made us incredibly efficient and networked, but they've also left us so disconnected from one another that James Challenger (1998), CEO of Challenger, Gray, and Christmas, is predicting that a new job title might soon be created: Director of Socialization.

Stop for a minute and consider the changes that have taken place in your organization and in your own everyday workplace experiences over the past couple of years. Many of us can recite these changes in our sleep. More team-based work, increased customer contact, multiple demands, greater workforce diversity, higher expectations, and tighter timelines are all on the list. While successfully dealing with all these changes may call for different knowledge and technical expertise in each instance, the need to interact well with others is a constant across every single change we make. Because of this, strength in Interpersonal Competence is moving front and center as a requirement for organizational success today.

Reframing "Women's Work"

Even though greater numbers of organizations are seeing the payoff from having employees demonstrate strength in Interpersonal Competence, one challenge remains that is particularly frustrating to women: Interpersonal Competence is often characterized as merely efforts to be "helpful" to co-workers or "nice" to team members. Labels of "helpful" and "nice" devalue important behaviors like the ones that ensure that a team continues working together effectively or that workers stay committed to a difficult task. The same "devaluing" also occurs when skills such as sensitivity and empathy are demonstrated. The very skills that help keep an organization running smoothly, keep a workforce motivated, and keep customers coming back are often taken for granted. Read through Activity 14 to get a closer look at this communication dynamic.

If any of the scenarios in Activity 14 rings true for you, or if you've observed any of them happening to women you know, you've had the

The Experience of "Getting Disappeared"   ACTIVITY **14**

DIRECTIONS

Read the three scenarios below and see if they are at all familiar to you.

- You're in a meeting and you get an idea about how to move the topic under discussion toward a great resolution. You put your idea out on the table—where it dies. Ten minutes later a (usually male) colleague offers the same idea and it gets scooped right up.

- You take on the leadership of a difficult committee, and through a lot of hard work, diplomacy, and the conscious inclusion of all voices and opinions, you lead the committee to a huge success. Afterward you're told how helpful you were and how nice it was that you "helped out like that."

- In your performance appraisal, you're told that you demonstrate some weakness when you're asked to lead a team. The "weakness," you're told, is your apparent need for input from fellow team members before you make a decision.

experience of "getting disappeared." That's the provocative term Joyce Fletcher (1999), author of *Disappearing Acts: Gender, Power, and Relational Practice at Work,* uses to describe this phenomenon.

Fletcher's work highlights what has been, for women, a frustrating and puzzling element of their workplace interactions. As Fletcher describes it, "getting disappeared" amounts to being ignored or trivialized for demonstrating relational skills such as empathy, sensitivity, collaboration, and diplomacy. Fletcher believes that these behaviors are labeled as "feminine" and as such are considered inappropriate to the corporate world with its emphasis on facts, numbers, results, and all else connected with the bottom line. Because of such narrow thinking, women who practice relational skills—the ones that involve connecting successfully with others—are dismissed and their contributions go unrecognized. Further, the power of the behaviors themselves is underestimated. But companies that continue to give them insufficient attention do so at their peril.

"THE KINDS OF COMPANIES we admire today are also those that depend increasingly on female attributes. We are in the relationship era: It's all about getting close to customers, striking up joint ventures, partnering with suppliers. Warriors don't make good CEO's in companies based on relationships. The new CEO is a Seeder, Feeder and Weeder—and those are women's roles."

—Janice Gjertsen, Manager of Business Development, AOL's Digital City, New York,
"Make Yourself a Leader," Fast Company, June 1999

What can you do in such situations? Remember that since relational skills are going to continue to grow in importance in the workplace, you are providing critical value when you practice relational skills. Fletcher (1999) recommends doing some "practical pushing"—pushing on organizational norms in ways that challenge them but that also "take into account the practical realities of being a woman in a predominantly masculine value system" (p. 120). Here are some of her suggestions to try the next time your contribution starts "disappearing."

- When you demonstrate relational skills, be sure to describe your behavior in ways that reflect competence—a language that *is* understood and valued in organizational settings. Describe your contributions in terms of the value you add to your organization. Also describe the work that others do in terms that emphasize the relational skills required to do the work.

- Whenever you head up a team and manage the effort using relational skills, consider how you want to report on your team's activity at the end of the project. Try summarizing the work in ways that reflect your own contribution as the team leader who was able to deliver superior results, as well as commenting on your team's contribution, which made the results possible. Reporting out in this way demonstrates the value you add and also emphasizes the relational behaviors you used to deliver that value. It also credits others who are part of the effort.

- Make it a point to name the contributions that others make in relational terms. For instance, when someone you supervise takes the time to ensure that everyone attending a meeting has the opportunity to state his or her opinion on an issue, let that individual know that you value his or her facilitation skills.

Practicing Good Communication Skills

Considered the core of good communication, listening is essential to Interpersonal Competence. In our faster-is-better business environment, perhaps the single best thing we can do to improve our listening skills is slow down. Slowing down lets us take in more information because we're really focusing on what is being said. It allows the person who's speaking to feel heard because we're giving him or her our full attention. It reduces mistakes and redundancy because we don't have to ask the person to repeat something that's already been said. As a bonus, slowing down leaves us feeling enriched because we've taken the time to connect with another human being. Regardless of how well you're already practicing listening, you'll do your career and your organization a favor if you resolve to be an even better listener, beginning today.

Another core aspect of good communication is getting the message across. Getting our message across isn't a matter of simply putting a logical sentence together and then delivering it to our audience. The message not only needs to be clear in content; it needs to take into account context, including acknowledging the person we're speaking to, the person's background and motivation for listening, and the situation itself.

Our rushed workplace habits that push us to be as efficient as possible can work against us when we're speaking. "Hurry up" habits mean that we sometimes take shortcuts in speaking—without even knowing it. Maybe we're not being as clear, as specific, as direct as we need to be. Or, maybe we're being too direct and abrupt, using only the minimum number of words required to get our point across.

When we're interacting with those who know us well, such as family, close friends, or colleagues, our shorthand way of speaking may suffice. But in our workplace communications, speaking in shorthand may backfire. Differences in generational styles of communicating, a growing problem in the workplace, can exacerbate the situation. Boomers and Generation Xers working side by side are famous for not speaking to or hearing one another correctly. Also, cultural differences, if ignored, can keep your intended message from getting across. The result is mistakes, hurt feelings, lowered performance, and heightened anxiety. Check your current speaking skills using Worksheet 4.

DIRECTIONS

Read each statement and put a checkmark in the box that reflects your level of agreement.

	ALWAYS	SOMETIMES	NEVER
1. I give my full attention to the person I'm speaking to—for example, turning to face the person, making appropriate eye contact, and putting aside any other distractions during the conversation.			
2. I make sure that my words and my nonverbal cues are conveying the same message. For example, in delivering some difficult news or stating concern about an issue, I make sure that my tone and demeanor match the message.			
3. I take into account culture, ethnicity, age, and other pertinent characteristics of the person I'm speaking to, and I make certain that my manner and style of speaking convey respect toward the person.			
4. I check with the person I'm speaking to after I've delivered my message to be sure that he or she understands the meaning of what I've just said.			
5. I make sure to use terminology that's clear and free of jargon (technical terms or "computerese") that may be unclear to someone outside the niche.			
6. Depending on the topic to be discussed, I choose an appropriate place for the conversation.			
7. Before sending an e-mail or leaving a voicemail message, I determine if a face-to-face meeting would be more appropriate.			

8. Before initiating a conversation, I consider any factors that might make communication with this person difficult.

9. I follow up on problematic conversations to determine how best to approach any future interactions.

SCORING/INTERPRETATION

- How many of the statements did you agree with? If you answered "Sometimes" or "Never" for more than a few, you may need to work on becoming more skilled at communication.

- You have an opportunity to increase your skills every time you open your mouth. It's a skill you can practice in any situation you're in; it's also a skill that you can always improve on.

- Consider reviewing one of the resources in the back of the book that give you a look at communication issues in more detail.

Expanding Your IT Horizons

If you are a high-tech worker who hasn't felt a pressing need to worry about this "soft skills" stuff, please take note: Organizations today are making it clear that workers need competency in their area of expertise *plus* competency in interpersonal skills. To perform well within your technical area and to move ahead, you'll also need people skills. Why? Because in today's workplace, it's likely you'll be asked not just for advice on technical problems, but also for help in solving business problems. Chances are also good you'll participate on some interdepartmental teams. And, if you're employed by a multinational corporation, you may be asked to help out on projects based in other countries, with customers or co-workers who have a different take on things than you do. So, as you consider your professional development, recognize that you'll need to polish your interpersonal skills as well as your technical acumen. Here are some suggestions to get you going in that direction.

- When you're explaining some piece of technology to a co-worker outside IT, talk in terms of what the technology can *do* for your co-worker's department or how the technology can help your co-worker more easily manage a new project, rather than focusing on what the technology *is*.

- When you're assigned as the technical resource person for a department, think of how your expertise could help. Ask department members questions about their business problem, rather than just listing all the technical maneuvers and bits and bytes you can offer them.

- Consider taking an in-house seminar on customer service or interpersonal communications if you think you could use a little brushing up on your people skills.

- If you're in a technical area and have aspirations of moving into management, consider one of the leadership programs tailored for IT workers that are springing up all over the country.

- Teach part-time at a local community college. You'll learn a lot about relating to others simply by trying to explain what you know to someone else.

Increasing Your "Human Moments"

Edward Hallowell (1999) reports a disturbing trend: more and more people are experiencing isolation, confusion, and anxiety as a result of doing most of their connecting through e-mail, voice mail, fax, and cell phone.

Have you ever noticed that after a day of telephone tag, missed messages, misconstrued e-mails, and cryptic faxes you feel some vague sense of being disconnected from other human beings? Or, as much as you love telecommuting and coffeehouses, do you find yourself missing the morning conversation around the office coffeemaker? Our new ways of doing business seem to be having some unintended side effects: fewer and fewer "human moments"—the real face-to-face time that used to be a much bigger part of our day.

Hallowell (1999) defines a human moment as "an authentic psychological encounter that can happen only when two people share the same physical space" and that requires "people's physical presence and their emotional and intellectual attention" (p. 58). Those two requirements mean that you must be fully present and engaged with the other person. Hallowell's perspective is that of a psychiatrist who works with executives, but most people I shared his "human moment" definition with nodded their heads in agreement and recounted their own stories of how fewer human moments were becoming the norm in their lives, too.

For working women, especially, opportunities for real, live human moments are at risk. Many women I talk with spend their lunch breaks, if they take them, returning calls to kids' teachers or coaches, scheduling doctor appointments, or doing household shopping. Informal conversation with co-workers, as much as they'd like it, is low on their priority list.

What's your own daily ratio of human to virtual moments? If technology wins by a wide margin, consider how you can change that. More face-to-face connecting will *not* make you less efficient, nor will it fritter your day away. Chances are good you'll find your motivation and productivity increasing. How about trying one of the following strategies?

SUGGESTIONS AND STRATEGIES

- Share your brown-bag lunch break with a friend, rather than sitting alone at your desk.

- Go to a co-worker's office to drop something off rather than putting it in his mailbox.

- Answer someone's e-mail message in person rather than online.

- Instead of continuing to play telephone tag with a colleague, stick your head inside her office and let her know why you've been trying to reach her.

- If you normally go for a short walk or run on your lunch break, invite a like-minded co-worker to go along with you.

None of these suggestions needs to take up a lot of your time, and you can still be quite businesslike in these face-to-face encounters if that's what the situation calls for. Just be sure you're really present and available to the other person once you've chosen to interact.

Networking—Twenty-first-Century Style

Not only can networking help keep you connected, but it can make a significant contribution to your career progression. It's a great source of career encouragement, which has been found to increase participation in training and thereby expand opportunities for managerial advancement. Networking can also help you get valuable news of stretch assignments and newly created opportunities, find out about position openings, keep on top of current issues and future trends in your company, and get assistance in benchmarking your skills.

Networking is not a luxury: It's a tool—one that is vital to women's career success. It does take time, but it's a matter of finding the right networking community that works with your schedule. When networks don't work, it's usually because of unclear or unrealistic expectations or a type of network that doesn't fit you. Clarifying your network goals and expectations will help steer you toward a better networking experience.

If your networking goal or expectation is to get a new job, you may be disappointed. Networking just for the sake of finding a job is much too shortsighted. If you are new to networking, your network contacts will probably be reluctant to tip you off to information about a new job until they know you a bit better. And, even if they do know you, unless you can tell them exactly what you're looking for, you're asking a bit too much of them if you request that they simply keep their eyes open for you. All these cautions don't mean you *can't* get a job through short-term networking; it certainly does happen. But it's probably a better idea to think longer term and more strategically. The better your network contacts know you and the more they know about your strengths and interests, the more likely they are to share news of opportunities with you. Why not think of your network as a long-term career management resource?

Aside from job hunting and seeking new opportunities, consider what your other goals are in networking. Doing so will help you choose networks that fit best for you. Is it social support you're after? If so, then networks like the ones formed by Dawn Gray in the Chicago area may be for you. Their brown-bag lunches focus on offering support to working mothers through discussions of topics related to nurturing children, helping kids with homework, dealing with sibling rivalry, and discipline (Gardner, 1998). If you know what you're after, it will be easier to find a network—or form one that works for you.

Also consider diversity as a goal in joining networks. Though hooking up with women similar to yourself can be affirming, you'll probably learn more by widening your network to include others whose background, perspective, ethnicity, age, or position is different from your own.

Here are some suggestions for finding out about networks.

SUGGESTIONS AND STRATEGIES

- Ask your women friends and colleagues what groups they belong to. What do they like about their networks? Could you go along with them to their next network meeting?

- Check out the professional associations you belong to. Many of these groups have regular network functions. One benefit of these is the participation of women across organizations and industries. Attending such gatherings is a good way to find out what's happening and who's doing what in your field.

- Find out if your organization has an internal women's network. Catalyst (1999), a nonprofit group whose work centers on advancing women, has recently published an excellent guidebook on the how and the why of establishing networks within organizations. Many networks within companies are thriving as they do a number of things for women workers, including educating the company and management on women's issues, developing opportunities for women, and creating a better workplace for women.

- Check out the organizations you used to work for—that's right, your ex-employers—who may have an "alum" network. Mieszkowski (1999) details a number of these networks, like the Microsoft Alumni Network and CNot, an electronic list of former CNet employees.

- Don't forget the networks available online through women's websites. Online groups like iVillage (www.ivillage.com) and Women's Connection (www.women-connect.com) have bulletin boards, chat rooms, and other ways of connecting that are only a click away.

Each type of network has its advantages and limitations. On the upside, networking with colleagues in your profession keeps you informed about trends in the field and about who is doing what at different organizations that employ people with your background. On the downside, colleagues in the same field as you may be reluctant to share information on new opportunities or positions because they may be jockeying for those same spots.

Networking with colleagues in your organization will give you a lot of important information to keep you up to speed, often on the unspoken yet critical ways that business gets done in your company. The limitation is that members may stay somewhat guarded because you all work for the same company.

Networking in women-only groups is often an affirming endeavor. You'll get lots of support on issues that everyone in the group can empathize with. Of course, women-only groups may keep you out of the loop on some information, support, and alternative perspectives that can be important to moving your career ahead.

Your best networking community will be the one that fits best for your current interests, goals, and lifestyle. It does no good to join a network that does early morning breakfasts halfway across town when you're on the road calling clients during that time or still at home caring for an elder relative before leaving for work. You may find that joining more than one network works best for you and gives you access to a wide variety of contacts. You need to take all these factors into account so that you can participate in a network that is enjoyable and enriching. And don't forget that much of networking is an attitude: Everyone you meet on a plane, in a seminar, or on a walking tour is a potential network member. Consider what you can offer in each situation, and you may be pleasantly surprised by what you get back in return.

Mentoring—Twenty-first-Century Style

If you don't yet have a mentoring mind-set, now is the time to get one. Why is mentoring such a big deal? For just about every reason you can think of. Recently I was part of a three-woman research team that coauthored a survey for the American Society for Training and Development's Women's Forum (Clarke, Kole, and Williams, 1997), focusing on women and mentoring. In our survey, we asked women about the benefits and skills they gained through a mentoring relationship. Ninety-seven percent of the respondents said they valued the sense of connection and support they received. They also listed the top skills they acquired through participation in mentoring: organizational and political savvy, communication skills, interpersonal skills for working with and managing others, financial and business development skills, and problem-solving skills.

The bottom-line results from other research studies—as well as popular opinion—emphasize the same points. Mentoring, especially for women who want to advance in their careers, is an essential tool: The majority of women who have succeeded in their careers and reached positions of influence credit their participation in some sort of mentoring effort for getting them where they are today.

Yet many women still press on without capitalizing on this option, often because of outdated ideas of what mentoring is or isn't, or because of their rock-solid belief that hard work alone will win the day. As a result, some women remain outside the mentoring loop and miss out on one of their best resources.

How can you tell the difference between mentoring "the old-fashioned way" and mentoring in the new millennium? While the need for mentoring is just as great now as it was in the past, the way that mentoring looks and happens today is significantly different. Here are some of the differences between the two.

Old Model of Mentoring	New Model of Mentoring
THE FORM MENTORING TAKES	
One-on-one pairings	Grouping varies in size
One mentor	Multiple mentors at one time
ROLES OF EACH PERSON IN MENTORING RELATIONSHIP	
Roles crystallized	Roles fluid
WHO INITIATES RELATIONSHIP	
Protégé/mentee was chosen	Anyone may choose
MATCH BASED ON	
Similarity, with protégé/mentee as younger or less experienced version of mentor	May be based on differences or complementarity between mentor and protégé/mentee
Chemistry	Commitment
STATUS OF INDIVIDUALS IN MENTORING RELATIONSHIP	
Mentor has senior status	Status may change based on need and purpose of mentoring
PURPOSE OF MENTORING	
To facilitate promotion and key assignments	Personal growth and development, as well as assistance in career advancement

Earlier versions of mentoring often had "rules" about who was mentored, under what conditions, and in what ways. Today, those rules are merely guidelines that suggest one possibility for mentoring out of many alternatives. Though the goals of mentoring—to share wisdom, knowledge, support, and critical business information—have not changed significantly, the avenues for accomplishing them have expanded dramatically. If you look inside savvy growing companies, you may see formal large-group initiatives, informal gatherings, mentoring circles, or small one-on-one dialogues. And chances are also good that you may see a variety of initiatives within one organization. So how do you get mentoring to work for you? Try one of the following suggestions.

- Find out what formal mentoring programs are available inside your organization. Check with women colleagues, ask your professional development program director, and read any written material your organization may have. Next, find out how you can get involved.

- If your company doesn't have any formal programs, talk to other women and find out if there are any informal initiatives. Women in some organizations get together for regular meetings, potlucks, or coffee to advise and support one another.

- Consider the kind of career help you'd like right now. What assistance would be useful inside your organization? What sort of help would enable you to polish your professional skills? What other kinds of support would be useful to you at the present time? Use this information to help you identify a number of people who could be on your personal "advisory board."

- Consider what strengths you have to offer. Mentoring is a two-way street and you have talents regardless of your age, life experience, or years in your field. Forget the notion of mentor = gray-haired pillar of wisdom; and mentee = young, unskilled apprentice in need of tutoring on the ways of the business world. The roles that mentors/mentees play these days are much more fluid than that.

- Look outside your organization for mentors and mentoring programs. Your professional association, your local women's group, or a civic group may all have some form of mentoring initiative.

- Forget any ideas you have about what a mentor should be: male or female, young or old, internal or external to your organization, and so on. A mentor is someone you can learn from.

- Check out some of the national mentoring programs for women that can match you up with a mentor or a mentee.

To capitalize on the benefits of mentoring, keep your thinking as fluid as possible. Your best mentoring arrangement may be participation in a formal program within your organization combined with a mentoring mind-set that lets you see every interaction as a "mentoring moment" when you can either learn from or guide someone else. And above all, try to get past the idea that hard work alone will get you where you want to go. You're probably already working too hard. And, besides, mentoring is too good a resource to pass up.

"AND LEAVE TRACKS. Just as others have been way-pavers for your good fortune, so you should aid those who will follow in your way."
—Ruth Bader Ginsburg, Supreme Court Judge, in The Book of Hopes and Dreams: For Girls and Young Women

Making the Most of Interpersonal Competence

Perhaps the best way you can enhance your practice of Interpersonal Competence is, first, to acknowledge that you have some powerful capabilities that can add significant value to today's workplace and, second, to support others who also demonstrate these skills.

Overall, strength in Interpersonal Competence contributes to your career success in two important ways. If practiced authentically and consistently, it opens the door to letting others know who you are, what you know, and why you care about them. It also gives you a foundation for honing your leadership skills, and, as such, it positions you for taking your place at the table where change happens, decisions get made, and new possibilities take shape.

CHAPTER 6

Flexibility and Savvy Help You Deal with Change

WOULD YOU BE willing to try a small experiment before you read any further? If you would, here's the experiment: Take off your watch and put it on your other wrist. That's it—that's the whole experiment. If you're not wearing a watch, try this instead: Grab a pen and a piece of paper and write down your name—but do it using your nondominant hand. Now, just notice for a moment what it feels like to have made this switch.

How did it go? Did you find it easy or difficult to adjust? If you're like most of the women I've done this exercise with, you probably found it a bit strange or uncomfortable, at least at first. Such is the nature of change. The experiment you just tried is obviously just a mini-change, pretty small in scale when you compare it with most of the changes we're asked to roll with in our work. Yet, the way you approached it probably gave you some interesting information about yourself—information about how comfortable you are trying something new and how flexible you are when making a change.

Flexibility is important to success because it is the key to handling change, the password of every organization today. Watts Wacker and Jim Taylor (1997), authors of *The 500 Year Delta,* have made a career out of helping organizations and individuals stay on the cutting edge. As they see it, "Successful companies are different every single day because the environment of the marketplace is different every single day. And successful employees will have to learn to do the same" (p. 253).

Your initial reaction to this idea may be to roll your eyes, sigh, and think of it as just one more demand on your time and energy. Or you may agree wholeheartedly with the authors but feel that it's someone else's turn to be flexible. Or perhaps you're like many of the women I have worked with who feel they've been flexible to the point of breaking and are at a loss to know what more they can possibly do. Wherever you come out on this issue, the bottom line remains the same: If you wish to succeed in your career, Flexibility is no longer an option; it's a requirement.

Flexibility is the ability and willingness to adapt—to change in some way—and let go of old behaviors, ideas, or ways of looking at life in exchange for new ones. This exchange may involve something as small as filling out an expense report using a new form or as big as adapting to a new reporting relationship after your company has merged with another one.

If you can make these shifts easily, you have a skill that is essential in today's workplace, where change is the only constant. If you can't make these shifts easily, you won't be able to take advantage of the ever-expanding array of opportunities in the new workplace. Or worse, you won't even be able to handle the ever-changing demands of your current position.

As women we possess unique skills when it comes to Flexibility simply by virtue of the lives we live, with their multiple roles, relationships, and responsibilities. All these connections require us to shuttle back and forth between competing demands for our time, energy, and commitment. And in the process we become skillful in mastering Flexibility.

Savvy, the second dimension of this Strength, focuses on understanding the underlying dynamics in your organization and successfully positioning and presenting yourself in line with them. In today's unpredictable business environment, shifting loyalties, changes in power centers, and large-scale reengineering efforts call for the ability to know and apply the subtle and not-so-subtle rules of behavior that don't show up in most employee handbooks. No matter how much expertise you have, you won't go very far if you don't have Savvy. It's as simple as that.

Flexibility and Savvy are combined here to form one Strength because, in many ways, they are two sides of the same coin. Together they focus on the ability to "get it"—to understand what a situation calls for and then demonstrate the most appropriate course of action. Mastery of both Flexibility and Savvy is necessary if you want to take advantage of the full range of opportunities in the workplace today and deliver the best possible service, product, or solution in any situation.

Mastery of Flexibility and mastery of Savvy require some of the same skills. Both need

- Some level of "substance" before you can demonstrate them
- Keen senses for appraising a situation
- The ability to continually adapt to novel circumstances
- An ability to apply multiple approaches to solving a problem or sizing up a situation
- A gut instinct for knowing when rules need to be followed and when they can be broken

Because Flexibility and Savvy share many requirements, practicing one often enhances the other. Learning to be more flexible helps you shift the way you present yourself and your work to better meet the expectations of a particular organization or customer (and this, in turn, demonstrates Savvy). And practicing Savvy means you can correctly interpret a situation and then determine the best approach to take, depending on what is most appropriate (which also demonstrates Flexibility).

Recognizing Your Innate Flexibility

THE LAST TIME Sophia came in to see me she said she had "lost it" at work, and she didn't know why. Somebody had moved the coffeemaker to another area and no one had mentioned it to her. Sophia recalled actually screaming at some of her co-workers about the incident. Why her out-of-proportion response? As we talked, Sophia began listing the enormous number of changes she had been going through at work. Each change required her to do something differently, do something more, or even stop doing something she had been doing for the past ten years. Sophia had always taken pride in her ability to be flexible, but the coffeemaker incident had pushed her beyond her limit.

Have you ever felt like Sophia—too worn out or pushed too far to be able to demonstrate Flexibility one more time? It's not unusual to feel that way. It's as though our "Flexibility reserves" have been depleted. And, in a sense, they have been. In times past, we were able to meet a request to change with a healthy dose of optimism and a willingness to be flexible because there was usually plenty of time to get used to the new situation—whether it was a new policy or process affecting our work, a new boss, or a new home in a new location. And once we had accommodated to the new, we usually had a bit of a recovery period before we were asked to be flexible once again.

But things have changed dramatically over the past couple of decades. One woman I worked with relocated four times within two years, just to dodge the downsizing bullet. Another went through three bosses in less than ten months. I've worked with women who have faced significant challenges from their work, their kids, and their partners all at the same time. What all these situations have in common is an increased demand for Flexibility with no breathing space between one demand and the next. If you're sensing the same thing, you are not alone.

With all these nonstop demands, we sometimes lose sight of the fact that we're actually doing a pretty good job of being flexible already. To better appreciate any changes you've experienced in the past six months and the Flexibility you demonstrated to get through those changes, try Activity 15.

Flexibility   ACTIVITY 15

DIRECTIONS

In the spaces below, record both work and nonwork changes you've been through, and describe the kind of Flexibility you demonstrated in each instance.

Change   **How You Had to Be Flexible to Deal with the Change**

_____   _____

_____   _____

_____   _____

What did you learn that might help you the next time you need to be flexible?

Sometimes just becoming more aware of our ability to be flexible can help us face future changes.

"IN MY LIFE RIGHT NOW, I'm involved with video stores my husband and I own, my job at a marketing company, and caring for our new baby. Probably one of my biggest strengths is that I am very resourceful, flexible, and, in general, a good communicator. I have to move between a professional environment (marketing job) dealing with presidents of Fortune 500 companies to a video chain with a very local atmosphere and also caring for our new baby."
    —*Elizabeth Lautner, marketing professional*

Listening to the Language of Successful Women

The words people use are usually a reflection of their thoughts and beliefs, and it's these thoughts and beliefs that shape how they see their world and perceive what opportunities they have in it. It's useful to understand this process—that our beliefs shape our language and our actions—when we listen to successful women describe their relationship with change and their perspective on Flexibility. Most successful women describe their flexible style of responding to situations in similar ways. They talk of "flowing with" the changes or of seeing change as a river that they step into. One woman made reference to being a "shape-shifter," like the mythical gods and goddesses who could change their shape at will to fit whatever situation they found themselves in. Another woman likened her style to that of a gymnast who could bend in the right way at the right moment.

This same language shows up in biographies and media interviews with successful women; their words are most often about "going with" rather than "going against." Few women speak of "forcing," "pushing," or feeling they have no other options available. Their way of describing Flexibility in response to a change comes across as a conscious choice. Discover what kind of language you use by working through Activity 16 on the next page.

"BECAUSE FLEXIBILITY AND ADAPTABILITY are strong points for me, I'm willing to consider new opportunities when they come up."
    —*Strengths That Matter Most Survey respondent*

DIRECTIONS

Answer the following questions.

Don't look at your response to just one situation—that won't tell you very much. Instead, look at your pattern of responding to a number of challenges or new situations.

1. What kind of language do you use when you talk about change?

2. What are the typical comments you're likely to make when a situation requires some Flexibility on your part?

3. Do your words reflect a "kicking and screaming" perspective? Or do you use words that convey a sense of challenge, learning, and new possibilities?

There are other patterns to look for in our language. Some bad habits that show up in the form of negative beliefs and words may keep us stuck in the past and unable to take advantage of the new opportunities of tomorrow. Have you ever caught yourself saying things like "That'll never work," or "I know how this is going to turn out before I even begin," or "We don't do it that way around here?" Phrases like these have a nasty habit of showing up when we least expect or need them—like when we're feeling resistant to trying something new. Catch yourself the next time one of these phrases gets in your way. Then resolve to change the way you're thinking and talking about the situation.

Being Too Flexible

Do you know the difference between being flexible and being *too* flexible? Successful women do. By paying attention to where they stand on issues that are important to them and recognizing their limits, they cultivate a "center" around which they can be flexible. You, too, can cultivate this "center." Once you do, you'll know intuitively how much you're willing to bend and adapt in any situation. That's the difference between being flexible and being too flexible. It's also the difference between bending and breaking.

MARGE HAS A habit of saying yes. Another assignment? Sure. Train some new people in her department? Of course. Stay late when she'd rather not? Not a problem.

Marge will probably reach her breaking point sometime soon. That, itself, is unfortunate. But Marge is also sending out a message that she may not even be aware of: She doesn't know when to say no and she lets people walk all over her. Maybe you know women like Marge, or maybe you are like her yourself. If you are, give some serious thought to why you feel a need to bend over backwards so frequently. Ask yourself what message you're sending out. And then think about whether your actions are pointing you in the direction of your best and brightest self. Your health and future career prospects rest on your ability to make distinctions between being flexible and being an easy mark. Answer the questions in Activity 17 to see where you come out on the issue of being too flexible.

Are You Too Flexible?   ACTIVITY **17**

DIRECTIONS

Answer the following questions.

1. Do you know when your plate is too full? When?

2. Do you know what you consider reasonable expectations regarding your workload and your performance? What are they?

3. Do you complete most of the tasks you set out for yourself each day? If you answered "no," why do you think this is the case?

4. Are you able to say no to unreasonable requests without feeling guilty or somehow less than competent? If not, why not?

5. If you asked your best friend for her perspective on whether you're too flexible, would she agree with your answers to these questions?

Sometimes those who are close to us have a clearer perspective on these issues than we do. For this reason, share your answers with someone who knows you well and see if he or she agrees with your answers.

Practicing Flexible Thinking

In the old command-and-control days, thinking for yourself wasn't high on the "must have" list for new hires. Today, however, your ideas and your unique perspective are just what is needed. As Michael Lynton, chair and CEO of the Penguin Group, puts it, "One person, thinking differently, can turn conventional wisdom on its head" (quoted in La Barre, 1999, p. 73).

Flexible thinking is the ability to look at a situation from a new vantage point. Women who use this technique ask themselves questions like the ones in Activity 18.

Flexible Thinking   ACTIVITY 18

DIRECTIONS

Think of a situation that is currently a problem for you, and use it to answer the following questions.

1. How else could you look at this situation?

2. What are other ways you could solve this problem?

3. What isn't being said here?

4. What's the opposite of how you normally would approach this problem?

Empathizing is another way to practice flexible thinking. It involves standing in another person's shoes long enough to get a sense of his or her take on the world. In our increasingly diverse workplace, the ability to empathize becomes even more valuable as we work side by side with others whose customs or worldview may be quite different from our own. If you can empathize, you will automatically get a bigger window on any situation and a broader view of the situation's effect on other people. Practicing empathy doesn't mean you have to agree with others or their perspectives. It does mean that you take a broadened perspective into account when making decisions or taking action.

You can practice empathy in just about any workplace situation these days because so much of our day involves interacting with others—as customers, co-workers, subordinates, or bosses. The next time a customer goes on forever with a complaint, or a co-worker is particularly short with you, or your boss seems on edge at the end of a long day, rather than jumping to judgments, practice empathy to get a bit bigger picture of the situation. Then decide how you want to respond.

SUSANNE WAS GETTING more and more upset by a colleague, Rachel, who Susanne felt wasn't holding up her end of an assignment. Realizing her attitude was getting her nowhere, Susanne tried to put herself in Rachel's shoes for a moment. From Rachel's perspective, Susanne wondered, might there be other reasons for not getting the assignment completed? Susanne recalled that Rachel had been putting in a lot of long hours lately. Could it be that she was swamped with other assignments? Susanne also realized that when she, herself, was under pressure she wasn't the greatest communicator. Could it be that Rachel needed clearer directions from her before she proceeded? The point of empathy isn't to try to second-guess someone's behavior. It's to try and see a situation from another's perspective. Susanne's ability to empathize gave her some new things to consider as well as some more choices about how she might respond to the situation. It helped Susanne formulate some questions and initiate a conversation with Rachel to get the situation resolved.

Broadening Your Perspective

If someone were to ask you to introduce yourself, what would you say? Chances are good you'd probably include some information about the city you reside in, the company you work for, the leisure activities you enjoy, and the community organizations you belong to (like your local church or synagogue, civic group, or professional association). All of these connections represent who you are and how you go about your life.

At the same time, your ties go even farther than you may realize. The age of interconnectivity that we're living in means that we're more connected with people throughout the world than we've ever been before. When you listen to world music, buy a piece of South American art, or wear an item of clothing made in the Netherlands, you're connecting with a world far beyond your own town or company. When you read a newspaper from another country, participate in a virtual team project at work, or exchange views with other women in online chat rooms, you're touching the whole world.

In business and in life, boundaries are dissolving and distance no longer matters. An article in *The Futurist* emphasizes this point: If you have access to education and communications technology, you will be able to "migrate" virtually, joining the estimated 100 million teleworkers that telecommunications expert Joseph Pelton expects to "roam the planet" by 2015 (Pelton, 1998, p. 24). With this in mind, if, in addition to seeing yourself as a member of your local community, a resident of your state, and a worker in your nearby company, you can also see yourself as a true global citizen, your world and your perspective will grow exponentially. You'll understand how your actions do matter on a global scale and how your perspective can make a difference. This is the Flexibility that will earn you high marks in your career—and equally high marks with the people who work alongside you.

Are you willing to be a bit adventurous to become even more flexible? If you are, great! Here are some ideas to build more Flexibility into your current lifestyle. Over the next month, try one or more of the following suggestions.

SUGGESTIONS AND STRATEGIES

- Go to a movie you might not ordinarily choose—perhaps a foreign film.

- Go to a section of your library you don't usually visit and choose a book that wouldn't ordinarily be on your reading list. If you don't usually read fiction, pick out a novel. If you're not usually a sci-fi fan, get the latest one on the new books shelf. If you've never listened to a book on tape before, do it.

- Choose a cultural activity that's new to you or a live performance event you've never been to before. If you don't usually go to plays, try one. If you've never tried the samba or line dancing, put on some dancing shoes. Check out that blues band you've been curious about.

- Find five new websites, investigate them, and see where else they lead you.

Whichever activity you try out, notice how it feels as you do it. Afterward, consider these questions: What thoughts and sensations did you have? What did you learn about yourself that you didn't know before? How can you use this new learning about yourself to further enhance your career? (Push yourself on this one.) If you have an adventurous friend or two, ask them to accompany you on some of these discovery trips. Then talk about your experience together afterward. It's amazing how, when we're open and flexible in one area of our life, our Flexibility often carries over into other areas. So enjoy!

Defining Savvy

Savvy is one of those mysterious qualities that are hard to pin down. Yet we all have a mental picture of what we believe Savvy looks like. Meet two equally competent women, Christine and Jane, and see what your impressions of them are when it comes to Savvy.

CHRISTINE HAS AN ease in presenting herself, a smoothness to her style, and a comfortable way of conversing with her colleagues. She also has what you'd call "grace under fire." If you observed her in just about any work situation, you'd probably say that she gets attention and respect.

JANE, WHO IS also quite bright, has something a bit irritating about her and seems to sabotage herself and her work at every turn. Her comments often seem out of place and she manages to alienate others every time she opens her mouth, even though her words are usually substantial and truthful. Observing her in most work situations, you'd probably agree that she's knowledgeable and skilled, but it's likely you'd also notice that other workers tend to keep their distance from her.

If you had the opportunity to observe these women over a period of time and then compare them, you'd probably say that Christine has Savvy and Jane does not. But how did you come to that conclusion? It's likely you noticed whether the women worked well within the unspoken norms of their organization's culture, fit in their setting, and attended to the political climate that surrounds them.

These three aspects are all ingredients of the skill we call Savvy:

- *Organizational culture:* the behaviors and beliefs an organization values
- *Organizational fit:* the ability to adapt to an organization's culture and a willingness to act in ways that accord with it
- *Politics:* understanding the way work gets done and the people who make it happen

Savvy is defined as a "practical understanding." When it's applied to organizational life, Savvy suggests the ability to understand how people interact and how work gets done inside an organization, along with the ability to act effectively within that setting. People who have Savvy somehow know the unspoken rules and the unwritten codes of conduct in an organization. And their actions show it. They know how to get their point across and how to influence others. They frequently have an air of confidence about them that earns our respect.

Demonstrating Savvy means paying attention to all these different aspects of practical understanding within your organization. For example,

- You know how to tell when the time is right to bring up a new idea with your boss—and when the time isn't right.
- You can sense when you sit down at a staff meeting whether there's some tension in the air.
- You somehow know it's important to greet that division head who's visiting from corporate.

Savvy is one of those skills that we take for granted and don't discuss a great deal; yet its importance can't be denied, and those who ignore it (thinking their expertise is enough to get them ahead) do so at a high price.

In today's organizations, a flatter hierarchy doesn't just mean shorter career ladders; it also means organizations that are running a lot less based on *power* and *control over* and a lot more based on *influence.* Many who make decisions do so without necessarily having important-sounding titles. They do it by empowering and influencing others through webs of informal power and politics. To get ahead in this emerging workplace, your career success depends a lot on understanding these underlying mechanisms of organizational life. In short, you need to capitalize on the skill of Savvy.

To get a quick reading of your Savvy skills, take a few minutes and answer the questions in Activity 19. These questions do not represent an exhaustive list of Savvy skills, but, if you can answer most of them, you probably understand the concept of Savvy and know what it looks like in your own workplace. However you answer these questions, the remainder of this section will give you some ideas on how to improve your "Savvy quotient" and further capitalize on this dimension of Strength 6.

Your Savvy Quotient

DIRECTIONS

Answer the following questions.

1. Identify three people in your organization or your profession whom you consider to have Savvy. What is it about them that puts them on your "Savvy" list?

2. Now identify three whom you consider lacking in Savvy. Why did you put them on your "not so Savvy" list? What separates the two groups?

3. If you really wanted to get your point across at work, how would you present it most persuasively?

4. Where is the informal gathering spot in the office for hearing all the news about what's going on in the company (perhaps in the cafeteria? around the watercooler? near the coffeemaker?)?

5. When you get a great new idea, whom do you bounce it off of first before bringing it up at a meeting?

6. Whom wouldn't you go to with your new idea? Why not?

7. Whose opinions are most valued in your organization?

8. What are the meetings that shouldn't be missed?

9. What are some of the unspoken rules in your organization that need to be followed and which of these rules would be the "kiss of death" for anyone who broke them?

10. What advice would you give to a new co-worker in your group who wanted to know the best way to fit in?

Understanding Organizational Culture

Have you ever heard a new employee say, "That's not the way we did it at our company"? (Or maybe you've even said it yourself.) Such a statement made once or twice probably doesn't mean much. But new employees who are fond of repeating this statement probably aren't bonding well with their new employer. Their inability to bond may be for a couple of reasons. One reason may be that they haven't yet been able to let go of their old company or its culture. Until they do let go and recognize that their work life at their old company is part of their past, they won't be able to embrace their new organization, which represents their present and their future. If you're one of these individuals, it would be wise to ask yourself whether you're focusing on the way life was for you yesterday or the way it is today.

Another reason employees may not be bonding with their organization is that they just aren't paying much attention to the notion of corporate culture. If they were, they'd realize that understanding their company's culture and acting in line with it are key to their success in their new job. Employees who continue to hype their old company's way of doing business, or their old department's way prior to reorganization, aren't demonstrating an effort to be part of their new culture.

At its core, corporate culture is what William Bliss (1999) refers to as "the sum total of values, virtues, accepted behaviors (both good and not so good), 'the way we do things around here,' and the political environment of a company." To be effective in any organization, you need to be Savvy enough to recognize and understand all the subtle and not-so-subtle cues that indicate what is and is not valued in your organization— and you have to determine how you can be most effective in that environment.

Lack of attention to corporate culture can seriously jeopardize your career. It can make you appear clueless or "above the rules" and can mark you as someone with little regard for the people and values that your company holds sacred. One of the dangers women face is that, in their need to prove they're competent, they isolate themselves and work like the proverbial dog, giving little attention to co-worker interactions, which these women feel is a luxury. Yet the very act of isolating yourself sends out all the wrong signals. Distancing yourself from colleagues can be perceived as unwillingness on your part to honor the culture. It can also mean you're missing out on an important support system as well as a vital network.

The next time you find yourself working alone at your desk when everyone else seems to be gathering in the lunch room, put your work aside and join them. You aren't going to sabotage your workday schedule by taking a fifteen-minute break, but you may sabotage your career by not taking that time out. If you're a telecommuter during part of your workweek, build some hangout time into your schedule. Pay attention to the time of day that people generally get together for an informal chat. Or notice what day of the week co-workers get together for lunch. Then try to schedule some of your office time around these informal get-togethers. You'll stay connected, you'll keep up with important company information, and you'll be giving yourself opportunities to build your Savvy skills in the process. You'll also be demonstrating organizational fit, the next dimension of Savvy.

Assessing Your Organizational Fit

Here's one way to look at fit. If your training, education, and past work history represent your professional credentials, then your abilities to get along with others, be seen as a team player, and display the right chemistry represent your personal credentials—your *fit*. And fit is a criterion that's just as important these days as any degree or certificate you bring with you. When recruiters or hiring personnel conduct interviews, the unspoken question that's on all their minds is this: "How well will this person fit in our organization?"

If organizational fit is so important, how do you know if you have it when you apply for a job, go for a promotion, or seek a leadership role in your organization? Information about fit is something you should seek before you even apply to a company for a position. It's also something you should observe as an employee looking to advance in your company. Determining the criteria for fit is a matter of gathering information before you go in for an interview, during your interview, on any visit to the company, and on a regular basis when you're an employee. And remember, fit is a two-way street. As you gather information about an organization's culture, also examine it from the perspective of how comfortable you'd be working there, how much the company values what you value, and how well the organization's benefits and programs satisfy your needs.

See the potpourri of ideas on the next three pages for learning more about a company's culture and values. You'll also find tips for making good decisions about how comfortably you'll "fit," whether you're considering moving into an organization or moving up in one.

In identifying possible employers and preparing for an interview, you could try some of these suggestions.

SUGGESTIONS AND STRATEGIES

- Don't start out with a stereotype of a company you're considering based on the industry it's in. Any company in any industry can be on either end of the scale or somewhere in between on such qualities as formality/informality, team-based orientation, and commitment to empowering its workers (Jennifer Chatman, quoted in Siegel, 2000, p. 257).

- Check company websites for clues to their culture. See what other information is available on companies at websites such as www. vault.com and www. wetfeet.com. (Siegel, 2000, p. 257).

- Find out the company's management style and compare it to your own. Are the two similar? Can you comfortably adapt your style to work within the organization's style?

- Use your network to try to talk with company suppliers, corporate clients, or former employees.

- Find out what qualities the organization celebrates in its employees and what qualities it penalizes.

During interviews and visits to the company, you could try some of the following suggestions.

- If work/life benefits are important to you, ask what kinds of work/life programs the organization has and what percentage of workers makes use them. (Some organizations profess to have great work/life programs, but in fact, few employees use them because the unspoken rules frown on such use.)

- Learn what kind of energy level the company is looking for in the position. Especially in start-ups—where a rapid pace and stamina are critical—determine whether your energy matches up with the organization's needs and expectations (McCune, 1999, p. 16).

- Determine what kind of risk-taking profile the company is looking for and how it matches up with yours. If you're coming from a small, cutting-edge organization where independent thinking and action are valued, will you fit into a company that believes in playing by the rules and not straying too far outside set boundaries (McCune, 1999, p. 16)?

- Notice the style of dress and level of formality/informality in the company. Would you be comfortable dressing in and relating with the style colleagues use (Siegel, 2000, p. 257)?

- Pay close attention to your surroundings. Notice the demeanor of workers, how happy and friendly they look, and how much and in what ways they interact.

- Try to interview at all levels and in all departments in which you might be working for any amount of time (Siegel, 2000, p. 257).

Remember that issues of culture and fit can vary from one area of an organization to another. If you're looking to make a lateral shift or go for a promotion, be sure to investigate how the area you want to move to does business and consider how comfortable the fit will be if you make a move. See the suggestions on the next page.

In my survey of working women and in my interviews with them, all seem to agree that when it comes to Savvy, retaining their individuality is just as important as fitting in with the organizational culture. Successful women are those who have managed to do both.

- Take steps to find out what the managerial culture is at the level you're being promoted or transferred into.

- Ask yourself if your style is compatible with what's practiced and valued in your new environment.

- As you move into more senior levels, the style and norms may be more subtle and nuanced. Ask yourself if you can comfortably operate in such an environment.

- In moving to a more senior spot, consider who can help you learn these more subtle ways of getting things communicated and accomplished. Consider who among your network, mentors, and sponsors you can discuss these issues with.

Traditionally, two big concerns for working women have been the fear of giving up who they are in the process of trying to fit into an organization and the worry that they will need to mimic the style of those who dominate the organization. One way to avoid these uncomfortable situations is to start out from a position of strength. Get clear about the kind of organizational culture that works best for you and lets you most easily demonstrate who you are, including your expertise and your personality. Try to do this early on, preferably before ever taking on a new job, a new assignment, or a promotion.

Having this kind of information before making a commitment to an organization or a new area will keep you from falling into a work environment that's not compatible with who you are and what you value. If the way a corporation or a work unit does business is so contrary to your way of working that it sets you on edge, then the chances of your succeeding there are next to zero.

Talk to your network contacts to see what you can learn about how well the company you're considering treats and advances women. Check the company's track record on "women-friendliness" with local, regional, or national women's groups. Organizations like Catalyst in New York City have information on the best companies for women. *Working Women* and *Working Mother* magazines also publish such lists.

Developing Political Savvy

If you're considering skipping this section because you're "just not into politics," please don't. Paying attention to politics, which is another important element of Savvy, is critical, and the following points illustrate this fact.

- When 826 HR managers were asked why they thought newly promoted executives failed within their first eighteen months, 50 percent of them listed "lack of internal political savvy" as one of the top six reasons (Manchester Consulting, cited in "Watch Out for Promotion Potholes," 1999, p. 1).
- Political skills have been found to contribute to positive job performance ratings.
- Management guru Tom Peters states in *The Brand You 50*, "All of life is political. It's well nigh impossible to accomplish WOW [projects] . . . alone. Therefore, it's to your profound advantage to master the Art of Politics (in the best sense of the word, i.e., cooperation and compromise in pursuit of a goal)" (1999, p. 75).

Politics are a fact of organizational life and, no matter how apolitical you think you are, it's critical to understand them as a mechanism for getting things accomplished. When people jump on the "no politics for me" bandwagon, they generally want to distance themselves from "dirty politics," the backstabbing, nasty underbelly of political maneuverings. That isn't what political Savvy is about. Taking the time to observe and gather information on the political climate and then basing your actions on those data is just another way of demonstrating a practical understanding of your organization. And it's a requirement if you want to continue to grow in influence and responsibility.

Studies of successful women executives by Lisa Mainiero (1994b) document the importance of political Savvy, or "political seasoning," as she calls it. Her descriptions of how the women she studied gained this skill over time provide some examples of the evolution of political seasoning. These women's ability to evolve politically was essential to their gaining recognition, respect, and stature as senior executives.

Mainiero found that the women she studied moved from "political naivete" (being generally unaware of politics), to "building credibility" (demonstrating their potential, forming alliances, and taking risks), to "developing their own style" (figuring out their own best way to manage others), to "shouldering responsibility" (being seen as a member of the senior team). In your own career right now, you may be at any of these stages, or perhaps at some point in between. The important learning, when it comes to political Savvy, is that your ability to understand it, use it, and benefit from it is a process. It takes time to become politically seasoned. But you can learn about the value of political Savvy and you can practice it every single workday. And remember, your success (however you define it) in your organization hinges on your ability to be a player who's recognized for her skills, her ability to make things happen, and her ability to be seen as a true member of her firm. You can't accomplish very much or make an impression unless you know the particular way in which work gets accomplished in your organization.

Accumulating Advantage

How's this for a provocative statement? "Whatever emphasizes a man's gender gives him a small advantage, a plus mark. Whatever accentuates a woman's gender results in a small loss for her, a minus mark" (Valian, 1998, p. 2). Whether you agree or disagree with Valian's remark, made in *Why So Slow: The Advancement of Women*, will depend a lot on your own experiences. But regardless of whether you agree with her statement, her work suggests that it's worth your time to pay closer attention to the way you are viewed within your organization, and it's wise to consider some strategies for getting fair and equal recognition.

Valian suggests that because of unconscious beliefs we all hold, women and men in our society are viewed differently. She believes that a problem occurs when these unconscious beliefs lead to gender-specific expectations and evaluations of women. For instance, if a woman is expected to act in a "feminine" manner in a certain situation, and those in power believe that she isn't acting in such a manner, then it's likely that she'll be evaluated negatively. (Recently, I heard about a senior executive at a multinational corporation—quite successful in her position—who was discreetly told that it would be better if she were more "womanful" in her style.)

According to Valian, one result of such differences in expectations and evaluations of women is that, in their professional lives, women and men don't start out on the same footing. Instead, she describes the environment as one in which men are consistently overrated while women are underrated and where men are often seen as fitting in, while women are seen as different. As a result, when a woman puts forth an idea, offers an opinion, or suggests a solution, it's often her gender—her differentness—rather than the contribution she's just made that gets noticed first. Seen in that light, her comments will be judged less important or even ignored.

Each time a woman is ignored, she loses ground and prestige. Worse, her commitment as a professional and her credibility are diminished. Every women who has made a contribution, offered an opinion, or suggested a solution only to have it ignored knows the sinking feeling that accompanies this experience. It's painful and embarassing. Further, it's damaging to her chances for long-term advancement.

Valian (1998) warns of the danger of listening to advice that suggests you shouldn't be too concerned about such slights. As she puts it, "That [kind of] advice fails to recognize that mountains are molehills, piled one on top of the other" (pp. 4–5). And while a woman's ideas are being ignored, she's also failing to "accumulate advantage," which is a critical element for anyone interested in moving ahead professionally. The result is a sort of double whammy. According to Valian, "A woman who aspires to success needs to worry about being ignored; each time it happens she loses prestige and the people around her become less inclined to take her seriously" (p. 5). Considering how hard most women work to prove their commitment, not being taken seriously is the last thing any woman needs or wants.

How does the notion of accumulating advantage relate to Savvy? Savvy is made up of equal parts observing and acting. Strong observation skills will give you critical information about how work gets done and who holds the influence in your organization. Acting in accordance with this information means you'll position yourself and your work in ways that will let you be the most effective—and recognized for your efforts. If you're ignored, then you're not recognized. If you're not recognized, you certainly can't be effective, and you probably won't be given the assignments, clout, or authority to make a difference in your organization or in your field.

What can you take from Valian's work and apply to your own career advancement plan? Valian has outlined a number of strategies that can help you accumulate advantage rather than disadvantage. Here are six from her list that have a direct bearing on Savvy and can help you hone your skills in this Strength (pp. 323–328).

- *Build power:* Participate in activities that are (1) out of the ordinary, pioneering, or not part of your job description, (2) visible to others in your group, and (3) relevant to your current organizational problems.
- *Seek information:* Ask about performance criteria, promotion opportunities, and other routes of advancement.
- *Become an expert:* Learn all you can about something that's valued by your organization. If you are knowledgeable in an area, it's easier for others to respect you.
- *Get endorsed by legitimate authority:* Endorsements don't have to be from an individual. They can come from taking an active role in your professional association or from heading up a task force or a committee, especially if it's a valued one.
- *Negotiate, bargain, and seek advancement:* Ask for what you're entitled to; ask for what you want. Women don't always do this as often as men do.
- *Overcome internal barriers:* Do what you need to do to gain confidence in your abilities and to recognize the part your hard work plays in achieving success. It's hard to build a track record if you can't acknowledge your accomplishments. It's also hard to demonstrate your strengths if you're forever doubting yourself. When you doubt yourself, you become preoccupied with *how* you're doing and can't focus on *what* you're doing.

In today's tight job market, organizations and leaders within them who overlook the contributions of women will surely have to change their attitudes and practices to make their workplaces more woman-friendly in order to retain competent women workers. But in the meantime, these strategies can help you better position yourself and your work to get the recognition you deserve in your organization.

Paying Attention to the Perceptions of Others

What's your guess as to how you're perceived in your organization and in your profession? The perceptions that others have of you, including your appearance, your reputation, and your credibility, combine to form your professional image. Appearance is probably the most obvious element, as that's what people first notice about you. But it's your reputation and your credibility that will determine whether someone sticks around long enough to hear what you have to say or follows where you lead.

If you've been paying attention to the underlying theme in this book—that it's a whole new work world out there—then you understand that the best way to succeed is to adopt the rules of this new workplace, which include viewing yourself as a free agent, constantly on the lookout for work that needs doing. If you can grasp the free agent perspective, you'll immediately understand the importance of reputation. The opinions of others you do work for will move you closer to or farther away from success with each project you complete. In the words of Tom Peters (1999b, p. 87), "I am as good as my last gig."

When it comes to building a solid reputation, there are no insignificant projects. Every project you do is a potential investment in your reputation. Imagine what you'd like people to think of when they hear your name and reflect on the work you do. Then find ways to make that image a reality.

Credibility is what assures others you are believable, trustworthy, and reliable. In today's rapidly changing and highly challenging business environment, this quality is crucial. Think for a moment about all the ambiguity and uncertainty we face in our workplace each day. In such a climate, it's the person who has a track record of being trustworthy, reliable, and substantial that we want to hear from. He or she is the one who will gain our respect. If you want to stand out from the rest and make a difference in your organization or in your field, you'll need credibility to do it.

Women often feel they have to push harder to be believed, trusted, and accepted—and that they must do so over and over again. Studies across industries continue to show this to be true. Often it's a matter of comfort. In male-dominated organizations, men generally feel more comfortable with other men, and women, because they're different, often have to go the extra mile—or miles—to prove their credibility.

Concerns about credibility get in the way of women's promotions as well. A recent Society for Human Resource Management study (1999) found men more reluctant to promote women than men into positions in areas that were new for them, even though these women were every bit as competent as their male counterparts. At issue was the women's credibility, which was questioned because the men who were doing the promoting had a lower level of comfort with the women. The bottom line is this: As more progressive companies look first at women's skills to make hiring and promotion decisions, women will be judged more on their performance and less on their gender. But, in the meantime, if you find yourself at one of those less-than-equitable organizations, there are ways to enhance your credibility.

Rather than put yourself in a defensive, needing-to-prove-yourself position, which does little but frustrate and drain you, why not focus on maintaining a consistent, professional presence that shows others your strengths and demonstrates your credibility? Activity 20 has some questions and ideas to assist you.

Credibility   ACTIVITY 20

DIRECTIONS

Answer the following questions.

1. Describe two women you believe demonstrate credibility. What gives them credibility in your eyes? What words or actions do they use that consistently reinforce their credibility?

2. Now describe two men you believe demonstrate credibility. What gives them credibility in your eyes?

3. Are there any differences between the men and the women in terms of what leads you to see them as credible? If there are differences, what are they?

4. What can you learn from these individuals and begin using to build your own credibility reserves?

Making the Most of Flexibility and Savvy

When it comes to Flexibility and Savvy, reflecting on questions such as these should help you make the most of this Strength.

Flexibility

- How can your ability to be flexible work on your behalf, and how can it help your organization maintain a competitive edge?
- When does your Flexibility work against you, and how can you become more aware in those situations in which you may be too flexible?

Savvy

- How can you teach yourself to pause—to stop long enough to get a sense of the undercurrents at work in your organization (all that information you take in that's not spoken or written down anywhere)?
- How can you better honor and act on this information?

By the way, if you're one of those ultra-flexible types, you probably still have your watch on your other wrist. If you do, feel free to change it back now—or not. Maybe you'd like to keep it where it is as a reminder of just how flexible you are! And if you're not yet one of those ultra-flexible types and you already switched your watch back to your other wrist, don't worry. The fact that you were willing to make the switch at all, however briefly, means you are open to the possibility of becoming more flexible.

PART THREE

Improving Your Quality of Life

I'VE WORKED WITH women who have ignored Quality of Life issues and managed to be brilliantly successful—in the short run. In the long run, they couldn't keep up the pace. What is saddest about their downturn is that these women worked incredibly hard and made huge sacrifices in their personal lives to reach a top spot or a key assignment. Yet when they finally "made it" they were often too exhausted or burned out to reap the reward of all their hard work or to perform at the level they needed to in order to make their new position a success.

You need to be able to shape a life that works for you on an ongoing basis—through busy times and slower ones, through rough spots as well as when things are going along just fine. You can't put your personal life on hold indefinitely. Your road to success has to include rest stops, periods of rejuvenation, and time for picnics along the way.

Women's lives today are full of complexity, with nonstop demands coming from all directions. Many women I've spoken with say they live with an incredible sense of time urgency from scheduling every minute of their lives. Under these circumstances, even leisure activities begin to feel like one more thing on a to-do list. When I ask women what they are doing to deal with this Quality of Life dilemma, many tell me that they make sincere promises to themselves to exercise better self-care, or to play more, or to connect more, yet they seem to keep putting those promises off.

If you are a working woman leading a full, complex, and pressured life, there are several things you can do to move toward a richer, more centered, and rewarding Quality of Life. The Strengths included in Theme 3: Quality of Life—Balance, and Coping and Self-Care—are focused on what you can do to begin living the kind of life that really matters to you—inside and outside your workplace.

CHAPTER 7

Balance Keeps You in Perspective

GEORGIA WAS CLEARLY upset. As leader of the day's program, I had just finished putting up some quotes on newsprint around the room to reinforce the day's topic—balance—and making some opening remarks to get the session started. Georgia had rushed in five minutes earlier and taken her seat. Out of the corner of my eye I caught her face, transfixed by one of the quotes I'd put up. As I glanced over again a few minutes later, I noticed that what had begun as a stare had changed into a look of profound sadness. Yet she didn't take her eyes away from the newsprint. Thirty minutes later, I called a break. I walked over to Georgia to find out what was causing her such pain. "I have to leave—I can't look at those words any longer," she said. "If they are true," she continued, "then what have I done with my life? I can't deal with the possibility that those words are true!"

The quote that had so affected Georgia was by author Annie Dillard: "How I spend my days is how I spend my life." Georgia, who had been putting her life on hold for more than a decade—stuck in an unhappy marriage, working far too many hours at a job that brought her little joy, and spending most weekends in front of the television—couldn't tolerate the thought that her pressure-filled days and wasted weekends had added up to equal her life. Her reaction, though more dramatic than that of many other women I know, is not so unusual. The realization that we're spending our precious moments as though we have an unlimited supply of them often brings us up short and leaves us yearning for a sense of Balance and wholeness in our lives.

Balance is both a complicated concept in today's world and a simple declaration of what we value most in our lives. What we move toward in our thoughts, words, and actions every moment of every day speaks volumes about what we hold precious—and what we don't. Balance, for all its current popularity, is not an easy quality to aim for. It's a truly personal pursuit, and a lifelong one at that. Practicing Balance means making moment-by-moment, day-by-day decisions about how you want to live your life. It also means looking at the bigger picture: how you want to move toward and shape a life rich in passion and meaning. It's important and essential for the twenty-two-year-old single woman who's starting in her first professional position; it's important for the thirty-two-year-old single parent who spends much of her time shuttling between two temp jobs, hoping that one of them will turn into something permanent; and it's equally important for the fifty-two-year-old married woman who's a systems analyst with a personal assistant.

Of the Ten Strengths discussed in this book, Balance is the one that falls by the wayside most quickly for women—not because of weakness or purposeful neglect, but because it's the one they figure is a luxury that they'll get to later, when the project is completed, the overtime lets up, the baby's in preschool, or their classes are finished. But somehow they never do manage to get back to it. Actually, the very act of postponing Balance in our lives makes it seem all the more impossible to move toward. For many women, Balance becomes a promise they make to themselves—a promise they know they can't keep.

Maybe you've heard some women say, "I've tried that Balance stuff—it just doesn't work for me." Or maybe you've said it yourself. I think there are a number of reasons for these "Balance failures." One reason for the "Balance doesn't work" proclamation comes from trying to plug someone else's Balance formula into your life. Each woman I work with has unique life circumstances: different passions; different priorities based on age, perspective, and commitments; and an individual set of values. All these differences mean that there is no universal formula for achieving Balance, and trying to follow someone else's model probably won't work for you.

Another common obstacle in our effort to achieve Balance is going for the quick fix: We get up half an hour earlier to grab some quiet time, we try to become more efficient throughout our workday, we skip lunch to get caught up on our e-mail, or we force ourselves to leave work half an hour earlier than we usually do. These are all great ideas, and I recommend trying at least one of them when things get a bit overwhelming. However, pursuing these activities and assuming they'll reward us with a true sense of Balance in our lives won't work. It's likely that we'll achieve a superficial kind of Balance—rearranging the elements of our lives like we're rearranging the pieces on a chessboard. But most often these efforts leave us frustrated because they don't bring us any closer to a satisfying, long-term sense of calm and well-being.

Usually the respite we get from a quick fix is short-lived and, before we know it, we're upping the ante again, hoping the new adjustment we make will have a longer-lasting effect. I know women who have taken the "get up half an hour earlier" route, then shifted to half an hour earlier than that, and then another half an hour earlier, until they are now getting up at 4:30 A.M.—but not getting into bed until midnight each night. I know women who forgo lunch daily or wolf down a fast-food or vending-machine version of a meal at their desk so that they can leave work by 5:30—or 6:00—or 7:00 P.M. These efforts are OK, as long as we can see them for what they really are: stopgap measures at best.

If we're really serious about pursuing a life that matters, we have to consider a truer sense of Balance by asking deeper questions like these:

- Who am I? Who am I becoming?
- What's important to me?
- How can I move in the direction of what I value in the short term? In the long term?

These questions can lead to a more integrated, deeper sense of Balance and to developing your own personal plan for moving in the direction of wholeness in your life. Rather than give up on the notion of a balanced life, I invite you to take the time to reflect on the questions raised in this chapter. Then determine how you can create a life that comes closer to what you'd like for yourself.

Balance is not a luxury; it's your life we're talking about here. Every successful woman I've worked with recognizes this and builds Balance into her life as a result. There's no reason you can't do the same. You probably already have some ideas about moving closer to Balance. It's often a matter of just getting clearer about your ideas and then figuring out ways to weave them into your life.

Facing Work/FamilylLife Challenges

"**MOST WOMEN WILL SPEND** 17 years caring for children and 18 years helping an elderly parent. Eighty-nine percent of all women over age 18 will be care-givers to children, parents, or both."

—*U.S. Department of Labor, 101 Facts on the Status of Working Women, 1997*

At the heart of the Balance discussion is the challenge women frequently face in meeting the demands and expectations at the work/life or work/family interface. How does a woman give her full attention to her job and at the same time give her full attention to her nonwork, family and personal responsibilities?

Many women today are closer to achieving Balance among these different spheres of their lives because of increased participation by other family members in household tasks and because there are increased numbers of work/family programs at work sites. Still, women, by and large, continue to struggle with this issue. Though some families have redefined the dilemma as a family or a couple problem of Balance, rather than just the woman's problem, many women continue to go it alone out of necessity or simply because they've given up on the fight to get support from others in the household. I still see an overwhelming number of women who struggle with Balance along with guilt, exhaustion, and distraction.

What can you do to achieve Balance in your life? Perhaps the best thing you can do is lighten up on your expectations of yourself. Remind yourself that you are doing the best you can and you're worth the gentleness and caring that you regularly extend to others. Next, try to get as much information and support as you can. Use the suggestions offered on the facing page to help you do that.

- Join an online working women's chat room and visit it regularly. You'll connect with other women who are going through similar situations. If you're new to these groups, look over the discussion boards and see what they are focusing on. You'll find support and answers to some of your difficult questions.

- Don't assume you know all the benefits and options of your company's flextime program if you haven't checked lately. There may be new programs or policies that you are not aware of. Get the latest information.

- Consider joining—or starting—a support group at work or in your church or synagogue where you can share concerns with other women and get helpful information about work/family issues.

- If you get overwhelmed, check your company's employee assistance program (EAP) options. Better yet, check them out *before* you get overwhelmed so you'll know how to access them if you need to. The support of a trained professional can help you sort through things you may not be able to see yourself.

- Along the same lines, find out if your company has a work/family director or office. They may offer support or programs that could help.

- Above all, do not isolate yourself. Women who are single parents or heads of household are especially vulnerable to isolation. They tend to feel they need to do everything on their own. But, when you're overwhelmed, your ability to think things through and make good decisions can decrease. These are the times when two heads are better than one. Having another person act as a sounding board can be really helpful at moments like this.

Substituting Work for Family

Eileen Philipson (quoted in Kruger, 1999), a therapist in northern California, has seen a number of them: women who have become so attached to the companies they work for that they end up with no personal life, no individual identity, and no larger life purpose to speak of. Nor do these women have any community that they participate in outside their workplaces. They seek counseling to deal with feelings of betrayal engendered by workplaces that made them feel like family—with team camaraderie, tee shirts, coffee mugs, social events, and close bonding—only to withdraw their "feel-good" attitude through layoffs, downsizings, or demotions. The situation these women found themselves in is not unique.

Today's workplaces present us with a dilemma. On the one hand, many companies encourage full participation, close ties, a strong organizational association, and a sense of belonging. On the other hand, they remind us over and over again that there's no such thing as job security. The result is a fine line between loyalty to our organization and a healthy measure of independence. And for most of us, most of the time, that works. Yet many women cross over the line and end up losing a sense of balance in their lives. This may have happened to you or to a woman you know. It's a difficult situation and one that can leave scars. Kruger's article describes the unhappy result: For these women, whether single, partnered, or married with children, work often becomes their sole passion and "the primary source of their self-esteem, recognition, respect—their only path in interconnectedness" (1999, p. 182).

The women "stepped over the line between what they do and who they are" (Kruger, 1999, p. 182). A number of women I've shared this description with nod their heads in agreement: Many know a woman this has happened to; some confess to coming dangerously close to crossing that line themselves. Philipson believes that this imbalance happens to women (at least the ones she's worked with) because they become addicted to the praise they get at work. Women can be especially vulnerable to this if "the workplace offers an emotional pull that may be missing in their personal lives" (Kruger, 1999, p. 182). And it's not hard to see how this can happen.

Hungry for recognition and approval, or sometimes just anxious about holding on to our job, we start acting in ways that don't affirm the kind of life we really want to be leading. For instance, we might begin putting in longer hours for a special project and then continue with those hours long after the project is over—in an effort to get recognition for our efforts. Or we might say yes to frequent out-of-town trips—hoping to get the approval of those higher up in our department—though we made it clear when we took the job that we didn't want to be away from home too often.

Doing these things for a limited time may make good sense. Our actions show we're committed to getting the job done. But continuing to do these things for long periods, especially when we dislike them and they seriously disrupt our life, takes a toll on our body, our spirit, and our sense of wholeness. Without even realizing how or when it began, we find ourselves leading unbalanced lives. For women, this is an easy trap to fall into. We begin acting in ways that serve others well. Eventually, though, this behavior—this doing to make it easier on others—can turn into a gift that we feel resentful offering. Or we may be so determined to prove our commitment that we begin making decisions based on what others want rather than on what's healthy for us.

Ask yourself how well you are attending to the nonwork dimensions of your life. If you feel that you have little time or energy left for anything outside your work, you may want to take a serious look at how you could better enrich the nonwork aspects of your life to maintain a healthy Balance.

Strengthening the Boundary

One of the downsides of our 24/7 culture is the unclear boundary between home and work. Thanks to technology, we can be available at virtually any hour. As a result, we end up feeling out of control and off Balance as we struggle to be "on" in every area of our life. But we really do need to take the initiative to keep work from taking over. Here are some ways to strengthen the boundary between your work and the rest of your life.

If you're telecommuting—spending all or part of your time working out of your home for your employer—make sure you establish a routine that works for you as well as for your company. Many organizations today are doing a good job of orienting themselves and their employees to the ins and outs of effectively working from home. But not every company has this figured out yet. Get clear on what your company expects and how you and your work will be evaluated if you telecommute.

Also get clear on your employer's expectations related to your availability for phone calls, faxes, e-mails, and so forth. You are not being paid to be a twenty-four-hour employee. Sure, there will be times when you're expected to be available, but make sure you and your employer agree on when those times are. These issues can be especially thorny if your company has offices that cross one or more time zones. I worked with a woman living and working on the West Coast whose boss worked out of a New York office. Her boss had the habit of calling her whenever he got an idea. But a three-hour time difference meant she received calls at home at inappropriate (and unappreciated) times. Unless you get clear on these issues, you'll always feel you're in "worker" mode, even when you're supposed to be relaxing and attending to your personal life.

Establish some time and space at home as "multitasking-free zones." At work, when we're in super-efficient mode, we frequently do more than one thing at the same time. We answer e-mail, talk on the phone, and perhaps even try to participate in a discussion with co-workers gathered around our cubicle—all at the same time.

If we're not careful we can bring this "talent" home with us. Suddenly we find ourselves going through our day planner or reading our correspondence while we're hanging out with our kids. Or we go for a walk with our ears plugged into a portable radio, catching the latest stock report while we do a turn around the block. Ask yourself, Do you really need to listen to the morning news and blow-dry your hair at the same time—on a Saturday morning? Do you have to check your office e-mail while you're sharing breakfast with your kids? Multitasking leaves little room for actually enjoying any activity we're involved in; we just end up feeling fragmented and distracted.

It's OK—actually, it's preferable—to slow your pace during your time away from work. Your family and friends will appreciate it, and your health will benefit from it. You need to give yourself time to rest and renew your energy. If you don't, you risk exhaustion and burnout. And you'll have a lot more to catch up on after a month or two of recuperating from your body's collapse than you would by simply allowing yourself time out from your work right now.

Deciphering the Language of Our Times

In our quest to achieve Balance, one of the best things we can do for ourselves is confront our cultural myths about the need for speed and drivenness. The media loves to remind us of the necessity of faster, better, more. Here's a sampling of some recent ads that portray hurry, hassle, and imbalance as a natural by-product of our culture:

- *Life is a tornado watch.*
- *Life is messy . . . clean it up.*
- *Tired of dragging yourself around?*
- *Why do you need a hand-held PC? Because it's your significant other.*
- *She went to aerobics, made four hiring decisions, called her son at school . . . and it isn't even 8:00 A.M. yet!*

If we pay too much attention to these portrayals of life, we'll come to believe that imbalance is almost natural! But rather than just nodding your head in agreement at all these life-is-frantic portrayals, why not see them for what they are: lead-ins to advertisements for a migraine remedy, an astronomically expensive vacation, a new couch, or a vitamin supplement. The danger in being seduced by these sound bites is that we unconsciously begin to believe that life is truly frantic, overwhelming, and hopelessly out of control. Such beliefs can be draining in themselves.

It's also useful to notice how we shape our conversations. Wendy Weirich (1999), a naturalist for Cleveland Metroparks, made this observation recently: "It used to be that we talked about the weather—that was the common starting point in striking up a conversation with someone. It was this conversation point that could always lead to common ground. But lately, we've shifted to a new talking point. It's not the weather anymore; it's the lack of time. Ask someone what's new or what they're doing and chances are good they'll respond with some variation of how tired they are, how busy they are, or how quickly time gets away from them. It's our new common language."

While it may be great as an icebreaker for starting a conversation, or as a common lament that bonds near-strangers, focusing on our harried lives does a whole lot more than that. It shows us what's central to us these days. The next time you have an opportunity to chat with a friend, neighbor, or co-worker, notice what you focus on in your conversation. Are there other bits of news about your family, your passions, or your hopes for the future that you could mention, rather than focusing on all the things that you aren't getting to, don't have, or will never be able to finish? Try it next time and see how it shifts your energy.

Moving Toward Balance

If you're like most of the women I've worked with who want to explore deeper Balance questions, there are three prerequisites. First, you'll need to stop long enough to create a space and a time for addressing these important Balance questions. Second, you'll have to be still enough to let the answers emerge. And third, you'll need to be willing to listen to the answers you get. We really do hold the key to our own sense of Balance, which we say we want so badly. But in the middle of our busy days and busy lives, we seldom allow ourselves the chance to listen for the hints that our inner source of wisdom is trying to give us.

Asking the Big Question: Who Am I?

When you ask yourself this question, make it big enough to embrace all of who you are, including these different dimensions:

• Who was I before?
• Who am I now?
• Who am I becoming?

Successful women think expansively. They don't confine themselves to such static, one-moment-in-time snapshots as these:

I am a twenty-four-year-old single woman, living in a very small apartment with huge car payments, a draining job, and a part-time school schedule that leaves me no energy for anything else.

or

I am a middle-aged woman with three kids that are growing up too quickly and a husband that works second shift, and a job that may or may not lead to something better.

or

I'm overwhelmed, running on empty, running late, in a rush, late on turning in that project, . . .

And on and on and on.

All these descriptions may well be true at a particular moment, but other things are equally true about the women making the statements above. These women also have hopes and dreams; they laugh with their kids, play with their dogs, and enjoy cycling and scuba diving. These life-affirming aspects can get left out of the picture if we confine ourselves to a static snapshot.

Try it yourself: Ask yourself who you are when you're out in the woods and the sun is shining through the trees, or when you're sharing laughter with good friends. Your answers will give you a more expansive view of who you are.

Activity 21 on the next page offers another way of looking at yourself that can be illuminating. The title of this exercise was inspired by the book *I am Becoming the Woman I've Wanted* (1994) and the poem "Finding Her Here" by Jayne Relaford Brown.

Determining How You Spend Your Energy

Sometimes we lose our way when it comes to Balance because we forget who we are and what we hold precious. It can happen so easily when the world around us is full of demands. Yet, if we let ourselves quiet down enough, we can usually remember once again who we are at our center. One way to get a good idea of how you currently spend your life energy is to reflect on how you distribute your energy among the various dimensions of your life. Worksheet 5 on page 149 will help you do that.

DIRECTIONS

Find a quiet spot and spend about fifteen minutes reflecting on all the things you're moving toward in your life, all the parts of yourself you're just beginning to explore, all the hopes and dreams that are part of you. Then, next to each phrase below, fill in any words that seem right to you—any words that describe who you are in the process of becoming. For example,

I am becoming . . . more playful.

I am becoming . . . more angry about injustice.

I am becoming . . . really good at my work.

Keep doing it until you can't think of anything else, and then try to add one more. Once you've done your own "I am becoming" list, reflect on what clues your list gives you about who you are and what you want to move toward in your life.

I am becoming _____

I am becoming _____

I am becoming _____

I am becoming _____

I am becoming _____

I am becoming _____

I am becoming _____

I am becoming _____

I am becoming _____

I am becoming _____

Discovering Where You Put Your Energy   WORKSHEET 5

DIRECTIONS

1. *Imagine that you have a life energy "credit" of 100%. This 100% represents all the energy you have available to commit to the four areas of your life: work, friends, family, and self.*

2. *Think for a moment about what percentage of your commitment and energy you devote to each of these four areas right now. Don't think in terms of hours per day. Think in terms of how much of your life energy you give to each of these four areas. Some of the categories may not be straightforward. For example, if you are a student, determine if going to school is mostly for career advancement or mostly for personal enrichment, or if it is for both. Then you may want to include a part of the percentage you devote to your schooling in the "Work" category and the remaining portion of it in the "Friends" or "Self" category. Remember to include housework in the "Work" category.*

3. *Now record your percentages for the four categories under "% As It Is Right Now."*

4. *Now look at how you've distributed your life energy among these four life areas. Reflect for a moment on how you feel about this distribution and record the percentages* **you would like to see** *in the second column. Remember that when you increase or decrease your percentage in one category, you have to adjust your other percentages as well.*

	% As It Is Right Now	% I'd Like to See
Work	_____	_____
Friends	_____	_____
Family	_____	_____
Self	_____	_____
Total	**100%**	**100%**

SCORING/INTERPRETATION

- Which area(s) in the first column got a high percentage and which area(s) got a low percentage? Try to determine the effect on your life of having one or more areas significantly higher or lower than others.

- How different are the percentages in the first column from those in the second? If the difference is significant, try to determine what it would take for you to move closer to your ideal Balance. What would you have to do more of? Less of?

- Remember that there are times in our lives when our percentages will be weighted more heavily in one area than in another. Special projects at work or extended caring for a relative will naturally cause an imbalance. There's nothing wrong with that. It's just a fact of life. A problem arises, though, when we maintain an unbalanced pattern over a long period of time. Such a lopsided distribution of energy leads to fatigue and burnout.

Char's life is an example of a lopsided distribution of energy.

CHAR HAS BEEN putting in a sixty-plus-hour workweek for more than two years now. Her company recently merged with another. As an HR rep in her company, she was given the difficult task of heading up a downsizing effort, and, once that was over, she had the job of reassuring the survivors of the company's commitment to them, along with integrating new workers from the company they had merged with. Most weekends Char brings home a briefcase full of work. Each time her friends have been able to take off for an extended weekend ski trip, she has stayed behind to work. Lately, they've given up even asking her to come along. Her ailing mother, who lives a mile away, gets Char's remaining attention. Char has put on thirty pounds, mostly from lack of exercise and a steady diet of fast food. Her only leisure-time activity lately has been crashing in front of the television after long days.

When Char completed the Discovering Where You Put Your Energy exercise, she listed 85 percent of her energy and time going to work and 15 percent going to family (caring for her mother.) She left the other two categories at 0 percent.

She knew this was terribly lopsided but seemed unable to think about shifting. "I'll let up when this new project is finished," she said when we talked a month ago. But guess what happened in the meantime? Three weeks ago, Char was laid off. Her biggest dilemma? Where to turn for support now that she needs it. Most of her friends have given up on connecting with her and her mother isn't able to offer any support. Burned out and isolated, Char has her work cut out for her.

Char realizes it may take several months to get a new position, get her health back, and reestablish her support network of friends. But she's committed to doing it. She also realizes she can no longer be the only resource for her mother, and she's finally decided to call an out-of-town sibling and explain the situation. Char has begun to see the light and feels she'd like to maintain a better sense of balance in her life as she moves forward. She has made a firm commitment to herself to do just that.

Completing the life energy exercise may help you gain a new awareness of how you're shaping your life right now and how you might like it to be. Awareness is always the first step in making any change in your life.

Reconnecting with the Dreams You Value

Sometimes life can keep us so busy that we end up putting important dreams on hold. These deferred dreams can haunt us, sometimes with thoughts of what might have been, sometimes with questions about why we didn't follow our dreams, and sometimes with wonder that we even had such dreams in the first place. Working our way back to Balance means giving ourselves the opportunity to get in touch with those dreams again. No, you may not be able to make the LPGA circuit since you haven't golfed in five years, you have three kids you want to spend time with, and your work schedule doesn't allow for four hours of practice a day! That doesn't mean you can't start golfing again, feel the exhilaration of the game, and enjoy the people you play with. Every successful woman I've spoken with purposefully gives attention to staying connected to her dreams in some way. Activity 22 will help you reconnect with the dreams you value.

DIRECTIONS

Find a quiet spot at home, or read the directions to this exercise and then go for a walk and reflect on the questions below.

When you've finished reflecting, be sure to write down your impressions while they're still fresh.

1. Think back to your early dreams. As a teenager or young woman, what were your hopes for yourself?

2. What did you see yourself doing with your life?

3. What was your sense of "living life to the fullest"?

4. What were the things that you felt passionate about? What did you want to be involved with?

5. Now reflect for a moment on what happened to these dreams. Were you able to achieve some of them?

6. Did family commitments or work cause those dreams to go underground?

7. Are there parts of the dreams that still call to you? What parts?

8. What good feelings can you get in touch with related to dreams you have fulfilled?

9. Right now in your life, what's your sense of what a life lived well might look like?

10. What's one piece of an old dream that you might want to incorporate into your life right now?

11. If you have already achieved some early dreams you had for yourself, or if your old dreams no longer fit who you are today, ask yourself what dreams hold your attention right now.

Our dreams offer us a window to what we're passionate about, and reconnecting with those dreams and finding ways to weave a piece of them into our lives right now is a sure way back to Balance. If your old dreams just don't fit anymore, then identify new ones. Given who you are now, what's your vision of a dream or a passion worth pursuing?

Making Elegant Choices

Author Marsha Sinetar (1988) gives us a plain and simple truth: "For good or for bad, we are defined and molded by our choices" (p. 25). But surely it's not our choice, we say—to work late, or to go to bed exhausted and wake up the same way. It's not our choice to be downsized or given an impossible assignment that leaves us drained at the end of the day. And it's true. Often, our workplace makes tremendous requests of us; and, more often than we'd like to, we feel obliged to go along with the requests—until one day we find ourselves leading a life that feels as though it were designed by someone else.

And here's the rub. Each time we acquiesce, each time we tip the scale in favor of imbalance, we give away a little piece of our life. Reclaiming our life once this has happened is not usually an overnight process. For most women, moving back toward Balance begins with deciding to make "elegant choices" at every opportunity. According to Sinetar, elegant choices are "those options that are, by and large, tending toward truth, beauty, honor, courage—in other words, choices that are life-supporting both in motive and in quality" (pp. 10–11). Though these words sound great, you may be wondering how they can translate into your every-day life.

Here are some suggestions to get you going in the direction of making elegant choices. First, take the time—five minutes, an hour, a day, or whatever is required—to become aware of how you are living your life right now, complete with the rewards and costs of your current lifestyle. If your life is lopsided and you are very dissatisfied with it, this should be easy. If you have only a vague notion of why you're dissatisfied, you may need to get more clarity before you go any farther. Then determine what new choices you can begin making that will tip the balance in the direction of wholeness.

For example, you can thoughtfully choose to excuse yourself from committees that no longer mean anything to you. You can choose to say no to invitations to get together with people whose lifestyle and interests no longer match your own. And you can choose to say yes to those activities and relationships that affirm and sustain you. From a place of conscious choice, you can make decisions that can help you stay balanced and centered.

You can also ask yourself, before you begin a new activity or move in a new direction in your life: Is this activity or this direction one that takes me closer to or farther away from what I value in my life? Even if you feel you must choose something—at least temporarily—that isn't on the top of your values list, you'll have a clearer understanding of why you're making that choice. And you'll probably make fewer choices that aren't in the best interest of your health and well-being.

Reconnecting with nature is another way to gain Balance in your life. I've seen this bond firsthand as a coleader of Reconnecting with Nature workshops for dozens of women over the past five years. Together with a naturalist and a cofacilitator, we've offered women a chance to get away into the woods four times a year. Each time the experience has been powerful, and each time the participants describe their hunger for this experience of reconnecting and the pleasures of slowing down, reflecting, and becoming renewed.

Reconnecting can take many forms: nurturing a houseplant in your apartment, starting an herb garden on your kitchen windowsill, feeding birds in your backyard, playing with your golden retriever, taking weekly hikes or monthly canoe trips. The point is to find a way that works for you.

Making the Most of Balance

Here are some suggestions to help you capitalize on this Strength even more.

- *Pay attention to the imagery you use.* If your image of Balance is that of a juggler whose hypervigilance keeps all the balls in the air simultaneously, then you're probably not going to immediately get in touch with any inner sense of tranquillity that reflects the calm you're seeking. Ask yourself, How can I change the imagery I use? What image—or photograph, painting, or work of art—can I bring to mind or keep nearby to calm me when I'm feeling harried or out of Balance? Am I willing to make a commitment to taking ten or fifteen minutes on a regular basis to use this imagery to bring myself to a calmer, more centered place?

- *Give yourself the gift of kindness.* Placing unrealistic demands on yourself, such as requiring that you do everything perfectly under all circumstances, creates imbalance and diminishes the way you care for yourself (Williams, 1996a). Ask yourself, In what ways can I be gentler and kinder to myself today? Is there one negative message I can stop sending to myself? Is there one positive message I can give myself in its place?

- *Explore ways to express yourself more fully.* Chances are good that there are many parts of yourself that you don't get the opportunity to express on a regular basis. That's just a fact of life for almost everyone I know. Yet a commitment to moving toward balance is a great chance to find out more about the many facets that make us who we are. Why not discover and get to know more fully these unexpressed parts of yourself? Ask yourself, What parts of myself are calling out for attention? My spiritual self? My playful, little kid self? My quiet, wanting-more-solitude self? What about the part of me that wants a more intimate connection? How can I express parts of myself that will more fully affirm who I truly am?

- *Notice where you focus.* We've all heard the old question about whether the glass is half full or half empty so often that, as you read it again here, you've probably already dismissed it. But back up a moment and read it with new eyes and openness. The truth is that what we focus on becomes who we are. The glass half empty means we focus on lack, on scarcity, or the worry of "not enough." You have a choice about where to put your attention. The choice to focus on possibilities instead of lack can give you a new vision for yourself. Ask yourself, Where do I usually put my focus? On what I have and appreciate? Or on what I don't have, but want?

Reflecting on the questions and ideas in this chapter should have opened the door a little wider to helping you think about your own vision of Balance. Remember that as your life circumstances change, so will your "Balance equation." The shape of your own balanced life will continue to shift and evolve. What is most important is that you understand how large a role Balance plays throughout your life. The next chapter, on Coping and Self-Care, will help you build on what you've learned about yourself in this chapter and give you some specific strategies for taking better care of yourself.

CHAPTER 8

Coping and Self-Care Keep Your Stamina Up

CONGRATULATIONS! After winning a spot on the popular game show *Lifestyles of Executive Women,* you've been selected as the highest-scoring contestant of the day, with the right to choose your prize from behind door number 1, door number 2, or door number 3. And here's the best part: The game show host will actually tell you what's behind each door before you choose, making it even easier for you. Your choices are:

- *Behind door number 1,* you'll find a week of dragged-out tiredness, mental fatigue, an understocked refrigerator, an overstocked freezer (full of microwaveable food), and an average of five hours of sleep per night.
- *Behind door number 2,* you'll find a week of stress-reduction and time-management workshops, a day planner with your appointments already penciled in (overbooked, as usual), an audiotape on beating burnout, a refrigerator containing some healthy snacks, and an average of six hours sleep per night.
- *Behind door number 3,* you'll find a week's worth of fresh fruit, two time-outs each day for renewal and centering, a map of walking routes near your home, a CD of soothing music, a personal address book with all your friends' contact information already inscribed, a bouquet of fresh flowers, and just the right amount of sleep each night to wake up refreshed and ready for the day.

Which would you choose? "Obviously," you're thinking to yourself about now. "How ridiculous do you think I am to select anything other than door number 3? Is this a trick question?" No, there's no trick. What you see is what you get. And yet, in real life, too many women lead lives like the one behind door number 1. Or they occasionally shuttle over to door number 2 but spend most of their time behind door number 1, without ever experiencing life behind door number 3. Why? Though the differences among the three choices in this hypothetical situation are clear, and the choice is easy to make, the daily real-life choices available to working women aren't always clear. At least that's the perception of some working women. They focus so hard on getting through the next twenty-four hours that they give very little attention to caring for themselves. When they do stop to nurture themselves, they often do so with whatever time or energy is left after all their other tasks are completed.

The way we choose to take care of ourselves colors every aspect of our life. The way we handle stress, time pressures, expectations, conflict, and the overall quickening pace of our everyday situations makes a huge difference. Our ability to find ways to nurture ourselves in difficult times as well as in good ones affects our health, our relationships, and our career success. Without self-nurturance, nothing else we do—not our educational attainments, not our over-the-top achievements, and not our most recent stellar performance review—can help us shape a life that truly matters over the long term.

And here's the bottom line: Women who succeed in their careers over the long haul have ways to both cope and nurture themselves regularly. The other important point to note here is that almost all the women I've worked with already knew how to nurture themselves. It was finding strategies that worked best for them and then making a commitment to themselves that often got them on the healthier, less-stressed path.

Strength 8, Coping and Self-Care, is more important than ever before. The pace, the intensity, and the expectations of today's work world ask more and more from us; that's just the way it is in the twenty-first-century workplace. To demonstrate your strengths you must be able to do more than survive. You must be able to thrive. And that is just what successful women do.

Coping, the first element of Strength 8, focuses on short-term strategies needed for handling the stresses and challenges we face each day. Self-Care, the second element, focuses on the long-term practice of self-nurturing attitudes and behaviors. Together, Coping and Self-Care represent an important path to enhancing the quality of our life.

MARCY, A STOCKBROKER at a large firm, went through some difficult times last year. More often than she'd like to admit, she would reach into her bottom drawer at the end of the day for her daily dose of heartburn medicine. When things weren't too pressured, she could go three days without feeling too bad. But during hectic, crazy streaks, she'd need stomach relief every day—sometimes even three or four times in one day. Weekends, she'd go into a frenzy of getting dozens of errands done as quickly as possible so she could play on Saturday night, and then she'd wonder why Sundays often found her in bed and exhausted until after noon. Finally, after eleven months of this lifestyle, she knew she'd have to make some changes.

A physical exam and attendance at a stress-management seminar were her first positive steps. Now, after six months of practicing some stress-reducing techniques, making a commitment to eating three meals a day, and actually using her Stairmaster for exercise rather than as a clothes rack, Marcy is starting to see some results. Her stomach is better, her need to constantly race with herself has diminished, and she's even started walking, rather than speed walking, to get from place to place. Marcy is practicing some coping strategies that are improving her health and well-being.

Coping strategies help us survive our hectic lifestyles and difficult circumstances; they make it possible for us to keep going, sometimes in the face of overwhelming challenges. Coping strategies include the use of time- and stress-management techniques, avoidance of burnout, the use of relaxation techniques, and similar methods. Making use of Coping strategies means you'll do what you need to do in order to avoid missing a meal, you'll take periodic stretch breaks from your computer throughout the day, and you'll learn and use time-management techniques to better organize your work.

Coping with Stress at Work

Even though there have been significant improvements in the overall quality of many women's lives, statistics and the everyday real-life experiences of most working women make it clear that women are still being pushed to the limit and, often, beyond it. If you're feeling like you have been facing more stress recently, you're not alone. Many women are experiencing increased stress. One reason may be that we've reached a point where chronic work stress (that's been accumulating for quite a while) plus personal-life overload (that's also been accumulating) have come together, and we've said "enough!" News reports tell us that women are even turning down promotions rather than add to their stress level.

Tension at work accounts for much of the stress we feel. As organizations push to do more with less, do it faster, and do it better than their competition, the pressure gets passed on to workers. When we're pushed to do work that exceeds our capabilities or resources, we experience stress. Below are some suggestions for Coping strategies to consider when you're feeling overwhelmed.

SUGGESTIONS AND STRATEGIES

- *Don't ignore the stress.* Unless you can say with some certainty that the source of your stress will let up soon, assume the situation needs your attention. Even if it will let up in a week, or two, or three, don't ignore it. Do something to take care of yourself now.

- *Remember that stress doesn't affect just you.* Work-related stress frequently comes home with you, whether you want it to or not. When Ellen Galinsky (1999), at the Families and Work Institute, asked more than 1,000 children what they would like to tell the working parents of America, one of the top ten messages the children wanted to convey was: "Don't bring the stress from work into the home."

- *Practice stress-reduction techniques.* See your EAP, wellness center, or physician for ideas.

- *Carefully review how you structure your day* and figure out ways to do your work that better support your well-being. Notice your peak periods of energy and when you slow down. Reconfigure your day with attention to your natural rhythms.

- *Rethink the benefits of hanging on to a position* that may be damaging your physical and emotional health and your overall quality of life. Before you assume you can't possibly risk changing jobs right now, ask yourself what you risk by not changing jobs. Talk to a career coach or a career counselor at your local community college. You probably have more options than you think you do. Women undergoing significant work-related stress generally can't see many alternatives. When we're worried or anxious, our world gets smaller. Our thinking gets narrower and we perceive fewer possibilities. Talk with someone who can help you see the bigger picture.

- *If you decide you need to leave the organization you're with* and seek another position, don't get caught in the trap of feeling that you have to jump ship tomorrow morning. That will just cause you more stress. Most women who reach a point of realizing that they must change jobs don't do it immediately. They put together a plan and determine their best route for making a switch. Sometimes just deciding to make a change and working toward that goal can help ease the stress you're experiencing.

Coping with Personal Stress

We already know that a significant amount of the stress women feel comes from home and personal life circumstances. For instance, though other family members may participate in doing the household chores, it's still likely to be the woman who manages the household task schedule: determining what needs to be done by whom and when. This management responsibility itself can be draining. For useful ideas on how to better handle work and family concerns, check out *The Job/Family Challenge* by Ellen Bravo (1995), executive director of 9 to 5, National Association of Working Women. Bravo offers strategies for creating a flexible schedule, suggestions for arranging a successful family or medical leave, and ideas on what your company can do to become a family-friendly organization.

The stresses that single women face are sometimes left out of the picture when work/family issues get highlighted. Yet women without children or a partner face equally challenging stresses and strains. In her article "Career Issues for Single Adults Without Dependent Children," researcher Mary Young (1996) makes this point:

> It is not necessary to have a spouse or children to experience the relentless tug-of-war between having and doing good work and living a good life outside work. You do not need kids or even a partner to realize that overcommitment in one area inevitably takes its toll on the others. (p. 207)

Some workplaces unconsciously marginalize single workers by focusing attention on work/family issues rather than on work/life issues. There is also, at times, a mistaken perception on the part of some managers that single adults without dependent children have fewer responsibilities. Often this perception results in women without children being expected to stay longer at work or come in on weekends. But dating, commitments to friends and family, time spent on sports or projects outside work—all these activities are an important part of the lives of single adult women. If you are a single woman who feels some of these strains, try some of the following suggestions.

SUGGESTIONS AND STRATEGIES

- Take the time to hook up with like-minded friends to share activities and support.

- Check out online sites such as the ChildFree Network.

- Nourish your friendships and connect with associations and informal groups of women who share some of the same life issues you do.

Coping with "Technostress"

Another reason we may be feeling more stress is that the ante has been raised by the addition of technostress—which, according to Michelle Weil and Larry Rosen (1997), authors of *Technostress*, is "any negative impact on attitudes, thoughts, behaviors, or body psychology caused directly or indirectly by technology" (p. 5).

Just consider all those moments when you can't access your e-mail, your monitor suddenly goes blank, or your computer crashes before you've backed up your work, and you can get a quick appreciation for how irritating and draining technostress can be. Consider these strategies for taking care of yourself when technostress hits.

SUGGESTIONS AND STRATEGIES

- Counter your frustration with some nourishing interaction with a real person.

- Put your task aside for a while, if you can, and come back to it when you're feeling more relaxed.

- Ask for assistance. Someone else may have encountered a similar techno-glitch and be able to offer a suggestion.

- Give yourself some tech-free time. Turn off your laptop, cell phone, pager, and anything else techno-powered that you're carrying. Even a couple of hours away will help.

- And don't check your e-mail during your tech-free time!

Shifting Your Perspective

Some of the challenges we face each day are ones we can expect, while others we couldn't have guessed at beforehand. We can significantly alter the quality of our day by noticing how we think about anticipated stresses and then shifting our thinking to better prepare for them. Stop a minute now and consider which challenges you can anticipate over the next couple of days. If you're like many people I know, thinking ahead about a day full of difficult challenges may go something like this:

6:15 A.M. The alarm goes off. You reach over, shut it off, lie there for a minute, and get your bearings. You realize it's Tuesday, the day you and your staff are to begin a huge project. There's that committee meeting this afternoon—the one where nobody seems to be able to ever reach a decision on anything. And tonight is that board meeting you're supposed to chair. And somewhere in the middle of all this you should be making some headway on the budget.

6:25 A.M. You look at the clock and realize that only ten minutes have gone by and already you're dreading the day ahead.

7:20 A.M. You've showered, dressed, and gulped down your third cup of coffee so you can get on the road and get into the office. With a sigh of resignation, you sense a gray cloud will probably follow you wherever you go today.

Rather than assume that it's going to be a not-so-great day, which is what you'll probably get if you keep thinking that way, consider how you can better manage what you know is likely to be a high-stress day. We're so used to handling stress with a "seeing it through, I can't do anything about it" attitude that we don't stop to consider how we could take better care of ourselves in such situations. But we do have choices. Here's an alternative scenario.

6:15 A.M. The alarm goes off. You reach over, shut it off, lie there for a minute, and get your bearings. You realize it's Tuesday, and in your mind you start running through all the things you'll be faced with today. OK, you tell yourself, it's going to be a heck of a day. So you ask yourself what you can do to take good care of yourself in the midst of what promises to be a full and challenging agenda.

6:25 A.M. Realizing you tend to tighten up on days that are so full, you decide to take a long hot shower and follow up with some stretches you learned in your stress-management class.

7:10 A.M. You also realize you won't have much time to eat lunch today, so you eat a healthy breakfast, going easy on the caffeine, which can give you a headache when you have more than a couple of cups.

7:20 A.M. As you get dressed, you reflect on how you can weave in some break time for yourself throughout the day. One thing you know you can do is take a walk around the outside of the building. It only takes about five minutes, and at least you'll be away from your desk and able to breathe some fresh air.

7:40 A.M. As you drive to work, you try to remember what's worked best in the past when you've been frustrated in those committee meetings. You resolve to practice one calming strategy that will keep you from getting exasperated if things don't seem to be coming together in the meeting.

8:15 A.M. You arrive at work, and promise yourself that you'll make the best of the day and let that be enough. You also consider what you can do when you get home after the board meeting this evening to end your day on an up note.

If you can think and behave proactively in dealing with the stresses and challenges you can anticipate, chances are good you'll alleviate some of the pressures you face, even if you can't get rid of them altogether. The successful working women I've talked with have all felt this challenge, and they have all designed strategies to handle the stressful events that they know they'll face. Try this technique out for yourself right now in Activity 23.

DIRECTIONS

Consider your schedule for the next twenty-four hours.

List ways you can take care of yourself during this time period.

Once you've filled in your coping strategies, answer the three questions that follow.

Your Schedule

Time of Day	*Ways to Take Care of Yourself*
Early A.M.	_____
Morning	_____
Noon	_____
Afternoon	_____
Late in the day	_____
Early evening	_____
End of your day	_____

1. Are these strategies that you can realistically implement?

2. What might keep you from using them?

3. How can you remain committed to using these Coping strategies?

Finding Coping Strategies That Work for You

Some Coping strategies work better than others do in reducing stress. It's often a personal choice: What works for you may not work for someone else. Some women have difficulty Coping because they choose strategies that are difficult to do regularly or that just don't seem to fit them and their circumstances. Your best bet is to know—and be comfortable using—techniques that fit the challenges you're facing. Consider learning and practicing a variety of strategies, including ones that can help you

- Relieve high-level stress quickly so you can keep functioning optimally
- Get through a rough day, time-pressured project, or overscheduled week
- Manage stress over a longer time period, such as when you're between jobs or taking care of a relative with a long-term illness

Knowing these strategies means trying them out ahead of time to see how they feel to you. Reading about strategies and knowing them in your head is not the same as knowing them in your body. Some will be easier to use than others. Just as it's a good idea to test your brakes before you actually have to use them, testing these strategies before you're faced with a stressful situation is a good idea. When you're in the middle of a difficult circumstance, it's pretty unlikely that you'll check out a library book or find an article you tucked away somewhere to help you get through.

In the "quick-stress-relief" category, get acquainted with some easy, user-friendly techniques that can be done just about anywhere and just about any time. There are many handy pocket guides that contain such techniques. Look in your doctor's office, the company wellness center, your community recreation facility, or various health and working women's magazines.

In the "please-get-me-through-this-week" category, aim for strategies that let you feel some relief throughout each day, such as those on the next page.

- Consider what you can do as you begin your day to set a calm tone. Breathing, meditating, slowly sipping a cup of tea, or doing some gentle stretches could help.

- Consider taking breaks throughout your day. Vary your routine. If you're doing a project that requires a lot of concentrated effort, get up and stretch every fifteen minutes. If you're working alone, take a time-out and connect with someone else. If the work demands lots of contact with others, try to get a few minutes of alone time, even if it's just to go get a drink of water or take a restroom break.

- Consider ways to make your time at home at the end of your day more restful. Soothing music rather than the evening news, a meal of your favorite food, a few minutes of meditation, or some physical exercise like a walk, a run, or a bike ride can help.

In the "stress-relief-for-the-long-haul" category, you need to aim for strategies that will help you over an extended period.

- Establish a routine you can live with and maintain, such as eating a good breakfast, taking vitamins, or stretching daily—anything that will add some quality to each day.

- Connect with at least one person who lifts your spirits during each day.

- Find some way of rewarding yourself every couple of days—with fresh flowers, good music, a period of quiet—anything that will refresh you.

- Designate a spot at home and a spot at work as a "quiet space" where you can go to calm yourself whenever you need to during your day.

- Simplify your life and your schedule as much as you can during this stressful period.

- Say no as often as you can to avoid overburdening and overscheduling yourself.

"**YEAR BY YEAR THE COMPLEXITIES** of this spinning world grow more bewildering and so each year we need all the more to seek peace and comfort in the joyful simplicities."

—*Woman's Home Companion, December 1935*

Staying Clear of Burnout

Burnout continues to be an issue in some women's lives. A decade or two ago the way a woman acted and related to others was often seen as the cause of her burnout. But the work of Christine Maslach and Michael Leiter (1997) has shown that the high stress and tremendous demands of today's workplace, rather than our attitudes and behaviors, are often the main source of burnout.

Maslach and Leiter suggest that burnout can stem from six areas of organizational life (1997, pp. 10–16):

- *Workload:* Is your workload manageable—or is it overwhelming?
- *Control:* How much control and choice do you have over the way your work is done?
- *Reward:* Are you appropriately recognized and compensated for your contribution?
- *Community:* Does your workplace respond to its workers? Do you feel a sense of community with your fellow workers—or does your workplace feel like a cold or hostile environment?
- *Fairness:* Is there a shared sense of fairness and respect among all workers?
- *Values:* Is your work seen as valued and meaningful by your employer?

What happens when people burn out? They become chronically exhausted, cynical, and detached from their work, and they feel increasingly ineffective on the job.

Some of the women I've worked with see their burnout as a personal flaw, and they berate themselves for not being able to deal with their stress more effectively. Maslach's work makes it clear, though, that burnout takes place in an environment where individuals are pushed beyond their limits over and over again. Your ability to identify the sources of your burnout can give you some idea of where to focus your attention.

Just as with other issues, however, awareness is only the first step. You'll also need to take some action to begin to ease the burnout you're experiencing.

Practicing Self-Care

While Coping strategies are essential, they are not enough. They are short-term skills aimed at helping you survive. Practiced by themselves, they probably won't get you closer to the balanced life you'd like on a long-term basis. That's where Self-Care comes into play.

If you look closely at women you admire—the ones who seem to weave their life into a brilliant tapestry, regardless of their life circumstances—you'll probably see a pattern. These women are highly skilled at practicing Coping techniques to get themselves through rough spots and keep from burning out. But they also go a step farther. They nourish themselves in dozens of ways on a regular basis. These women thrive by adding Self-Care rituals to their Coping strategies to keep themselves healthy and fully engaged in their life. And, in addition to enriching their personal life, women who practice these "thrival" strategies bring creativity, resilience, and aliveness to their professional life.

One way to thrive is through play—with your children, your pets, your friends, your partner, your neighbors' kids. Playing is serious business. Do you have a workout routine? Physical activity and play can do more for your health than you may imagine. Often, physical exercise and play can renew, motivate, and inspire us.

For some women, play takes the form of a family vacation—which mom plans for, shops for, and makes all the arrangements for. Or play becomes an event that we look forward to once or twice a year. That's not enough. Play, leisure pursuits, and physical activity need to be an integral part of your life—something woven into your everyday experience.

Drop the words "if only" from your vocabulary immediately. Every moment we waste on "if only I had time . . ." or "once I accomplish . . ." or "after I'm vested . . ." robs us of the richness of the present. What would your life be like if you were totally alive in the present moment? Chances are good your senses would be more alive, your openness to possibilities would increase, and you'd be awake in a way you've never before experienced. Women I've talked with who have "made friends with time" report the sensation of feeling time stand still. How? They become so involved with what they are doing that they don't glance at a clock or consider whether they should be doing something else. They garden, or mold clay, or play an instrument, or give their child a bath. They attend to every single moment of the experience—what the air smells like, or what their child's skin feels like, or what a bird in a nearby tree sounds like. That awareness wakes them up in ways that seem to slow time down for them—quite the opposite of what we usually feel.

One of the downsides to our current pace of life is that qualities like beauty and pleasure are often forgotten—there seems to be no time to weave them into our everyday routine. When you're going full speed ahead, the "little things" usually get left behind—things like the joy of arranging fresh flowers, the sound of soothing music, or the feel of a really good massage. Yet these are the things that can sustain us. Remember Marcy, the stressed-out stockbroker from earlier in this chapter?

ONCE MARCY SAW the damage that her stressed-out lifestyle was inflicting on her health and quality of life, she began practicing some good Coping strategies. But, though she experienced some stress relief, she also noticed that she wasn't experiencing much joy—just less stress. We talked about what she could do to bring more joy into her life. And Marcy made a plan. Weekends now begin with a walk around her condo complex. On the walks, she focuses on the sounds and sights around her. Marcy also puts a limit to her errand running: no more than five errand stops at a time. She discovered a nearby vegetarian restaurant that's become her favorite place for lunch on Saturdays. She's also started getting to know her neighbors in the adjoining condos. Connecting with others has become pleasurable, and she automatically slows down when she stops to chat with them. Marcy has started to weave Self-Care into her life.

Developing Your Support Network

When I surveyed hundreds of working women, asking them what factors contributed to their success and what factors got in their way, support system was mentioned almost every time. In about two-thirds of the cases, women attributed their success, in large part, to the support they received from others; and in about one-third of the cases, lack of a support system came up as one of the top obstacles to a woman's success.

Those women who lacked support generally explained their situation in one of two ways: Either a woman felt she had no one she could turn to (the situation of many single heads of households) or she had family and/or friends who disapproved of her career pursuit and told her so or withdrew their support for her at critical times. The consequence of either situation was that these women lacked a supportive base that offered encouragement, advice, and connection.

If you feel a lack of support to pursue your dreams, find and create a circle of people who care about you. Dreams die in isolation, and everyday challenges can seem overwhelming. If your family can't support and encourage you, find people who can. If you're new to an area, begin now to tap into networks that you can be a part of, where you can receive support and offer it to other women.

Women who succeed and thrive have a support system. They also understand the value of nurturing that support system every bit as much as they attend to their professional network. Just as Tom Peters (1999a) emphasizes "You are your network," the corollary is also true: You are your support system.

Women can become isolated as work takes up more and more hours and time after work turns into errands and chores. The support of a community of like-minded souls can't be underestimated. Whom do you consider to be part of your community? Your neighbors? Church or synagogue members? Perhaps parents of the children your kids pal around with?

If none of these is an option, there are other ways of building community. Environmental movements, human rights movements, sports, and the arts have communities of their own. One value of communities like these outside the workplace is that your participation in them lets you develop a sense of yourself outside your professional role. Participation in community theater, a gardening club, or a church choir reminds you that you are a multifaceted, multitalented woman. And given how hard most women work at their professional role, it's important to be affirmed for all of who you are, not just who you are at work. If you don't belong to a community group, you may want to check out some of the following suggestions.

- What interests do you have that you'd like to learn more about? What would you like to play at? Ask yourself how you might pursue one interest.

- Check your hometown newspaper for local community gatherings. Your local cable station may have information on what's happening nearby.

- Look in your phone book for listings of local chapters of groups or causes you're interested in. Go to a couple of meetings of different groups. See which ones feel like a good fit for you.

- If participating in a community doesn't seem possible right now, how about chat rooms and participating in an online one instead? Online virtual communities are growing, especially at women-focused websites. Chances are good that if you have an interest, there's not only a website that covers it, but also a community of like-minded others.

It takes time and practice for Coping and Self-Care strategies to make a difference in your life. Your commitment to trying these strategies over an extended period will be a huge contributor to changing the quality of your life for the better. In the same way that you wouldn't think of leaving home without your keys, identification, or other important material you need to get your work accomplished each day, it's just as important to take your favorite Coping and Self-Care strategies with you wherever you go.

Making the Most of Coping and Self-Care

What do you intend to do with whatever time you free up for yourself? It's easy to lose sight of the fact that your goal isn't to free up more time so you can do more work—your goal is to enrich and deepen the quality of your life. How do you plan to spend your gift of more time?

Ask yourself what keeps you from nurturing yourself. What would happen if you truly saw yourself as worthy of tenderness and gentle care? What strengths can you bring to your work when you're feeling rested, more centered, and true to yourself?

PART FOUR

Keeping Focused on the Big Picture

HOW BIG WOULD you say your picture of the future is right now? When it comes to your career advancement and the possible pathways you might pursue to move forward, how many possible scenarios are you willing to entertain? Your ability to envision several possible futures and several paths to get you there is a key strength.

Theme Four focuses on the big-picture view that opens the door wide to a full range of possible ways you can go forward successfully in your career. The Big Picture includes attention to and participation in our expanding e-world. Without a doubt, that's where we're heading. As Ling Chai, founder and president of Jenzabar.com (quoted in McCauley, 1999) points out,

> we need to make sure that we don't let the world define who we are. We need to define those things for ourselves. A big part of that self-definition involves our relationship with technology. The Internet is poised to change how we work and live. . . . If we aren't equal participants in the Net, we risk re-creating all of the problems that we've experienced throughout the 20th century. (p. 108)

The time and energy you invest in becoming techno-smart will pay off for you in ways you can't even predict today. So, take the e-world into account as you shape your career and your future. Read up on the lives and careers of women who have embraced technology, such as Aliza Sherman, who created Cybergrrls, and Grace Hopper, a prominent computer science pioneer. Learn about the women in the sciences who are making a difference in the world and challenge yourself to do the same.

The Strengths in Theme Four: The Big Picture—Awareness of Opportunities and Creativity and Leadership—will help you explore possibilities for your future and will also challenge you to identify and build on your strengths to go after these possibilities. In the days ahead, Awareness of Opportunities and your ability to use your Creativity and your Leadership skills to capitalize on them will make all the difference. It doesn't matter if you're in IT, health care, education, or financial services; it's your ability to see the Big Picture, see yourself as a potential leader, and move yourself toward that vision that matters most.

As a working woman in this new century, your future is bright. Why not appraise your opportunities and choose the ones where you can be an agent of change and make a difference—in your life and in the direction of your organization. Theme Four will point you in the right direction to do just that.

CHAPTER 9

Awareness of Opportunities Increases Your Options

READ THESE VIGNETTES and then consider how you would answer the questions that follow them.

QUITE UNEXPECTEDLY, Kristin just got downsized. She figures now is as good a time as any to travel through Mexico—something she's always wanted to do.

GENEVA WAS going to go back to school this year but her boss just offered her another raise. So she figures she'll put off school for at least another six months and stay with her job for now.

MONA FINALLY got fed up enough with her negative supervisor to request a transfer to another area.

DONNA'S DREAM came true when she got the promotion she had been preparing for during the past year and a half.

LALEI'S DREAMS of an acting career in New York City aren't being realized. She's considering a move to the West Coast to see what opportunities she might find there.

Here are the questions:

• Which of these women appears to be seizing a career opportunity?
• Which is more likely to advance in the days ahead?
• Which one has painted herself into a corner?

And the answers?

The long answer is that all five women stand an equal chance of seizing a career opportunity, advancing in the days ahead, or painting themselves into a corner. The short answer is that it all depends. It depends on the way in which each woman views her situation, appraises its possibilities, and uses it to her advantage.

Opportunities, like many other things in life, are often seen as such only in the eyes of the beholder. What's an opportunity to one woman may seem like a step backward to another. What looks like a plum assignment to one worker may look like too high a risk to someone else. How you choose to interpret the opportunities that are out there and whether you capitalize on them will make all the difference in your career success. Right now, at this very moment, there are dozens of opportunities all around you. But the likelihood that you'll take full advantage of them depends on your ability to practice Strength 9, Awareness of Opportunities. Like all the other Strengths, this one takes effort on your part—effort that will definitely enhance your career.

"I HAD TO MAKE MY OWN living and my own opportunity.... Don't sit down and wait for the opportunities to come: You have to get up and make them."
—*Madame C. J. Walker, entrepreneur, philanthropist, and social activist, in* Voices of the Dream: African American Women Speak

Positioning Yourself to Take Advantage of Opportunities

Preparing yourself to profit from opportunities—both the ones that come to you and the ones you create—requires the right attitude and the right information about your range of options. You can get both by doing the following:

• *Cultivating your curiosity:* Are you one of those women who always wonders what's just around the next corner? Who loves new ideas?

Who tends to notice things others don't? If you are, then you're a natural at practicing Awareness of Opportunities. If you're not, consider how you can expand your curiosity. Without a doubt, it's the curious, the opportunity-minded, and the enterprising women who stand to gain the most in today's workplace. Why? Because curiosity leads to the discovery of opportunities, and opportunities are the passport to success for both individuals and corporations in the new economy.

- *"Branding" yourself:* Now is the time to get out every bit of self-assessment work you've done on yourself from the previous chapters of this book. Use this material to create "Brand You"—that combination of skills and talent that enables you to offer your products and services in a way that absolutely nobody else can.
- *Cashing in on the work that needs doing:* The focus throughout this book has been on encouraging you to think less about job titles and more about work that needs doing. If you're serious about building your career, you'll find that uncovering opportunities is key to your success. By investing your time, energy, and effort in imagining possibilities that may be just taking shape on the horizon, you increase your own options considerably. The sections that follow will get you thinking more in this new way.

Assessing the Value of Opportunities

Anyone can brag about spotting opportunities, but following through and making the most of the good ones will set you apart as an opportunity maker. All the opportunities in the world won't get you anywhere if you aren't able to capitalize on them. I've worked with women who can easily spot opportunities or point out a trend and describe how it might be turned into an opportunity. Yet some of these same women can't seem to take the next critical step: converting the opportunity they've identified into an advantage in their own career. Perhaps this has even happened to you. You get a great idea or an opportunity comes knocking at your door—but you don't answer it. Why not?

Elizabeth Williams and her colleagues (1998) examined the career paths of professional women, and their work sheds some light on this

"Why not?" question. They identified some "readiness factors" in the professionals they studied that often determined whether a woman capitalized on an opportunity. Though their research focused on women's ability to take advantage of opportunities they hadn't planned for—what the researchers called "chance events"—the readiness factors they identified are relevant for just about every situation. The researchers found that two groups of factors—external and internal readiness factors—made the difference. Women who possessed internal readiness factors such as confidence, self-efficacy, an ability to take risks, a willingness to be adventurous, and flexibility, along with the external readiness factor of support from others—all factors that reflect the Strengths described in this book—were able to capitalize on opportunities. Women who didn't possess these traits couldn't do that.

The researchers identified another external factor: timing. They found that timing helped determine whether a woman acted on an opportunity, suggesting that being "in the right place at the right time" really could be a catalyst for profiting from an opportunity. But timing is an advantage only if, in addition to being in the right place at the right time, you also show up with the right talent.

The work of Williams and her colleagues suggests that it takes a solid foundation, built by practicing skills like the Strengths described in this book, to feel ready to take the leap of faith that seizing opportunities requires. Without that foundation, you'll never be ready to act on the opportunities you identify.

Before you go for that opportunity, though, it's probably a good idea to take a closer look at it. Taking on more responsibility without a corresponding increase in power, recognition, or compensation isn't necessarily such a great opportunity. Women who are prone to saying yes to any and all requests from others (and this is especially true for women in the helping professions) are also prone to accepting opportunities that do nothing more than give them more work for the same pay. There are other women who don't want to turn down any opportunity, for fear it will take them out of the running. Does either of these profiles describe you? If so, be cautious. Saying yes to anything that's offered means you'll have neither the time nor the energy left for the plum assignments you do want to take on when they're offered to you.

KELLY MADE IT a policy to say yes to any assignment she was offered. Her reasoning went something like this: "If I turn it down, I won't appear motivated. I want people to see me as promotable. And, anyway, it will look good on my résumé to add one more skill." Actually, Kelly was giving the opposite impression. If no one else wanted to take on another assignment, word was out that Kelly would do it. Kelly was sabotaging herself and exhausting herself in the process.

While it's likely that you won't know the total payoff of seizing an opportunity beforehand, it's still worth your effort to check it out as much as you can before jumping in. Try putting your opportunity to the test in Activity 24. You may not be able to answer all these questions, but you should be able to understand the value of the potential opportunity a bit more after you've gone through this checklist. And once you get in the habit of appraising opportunities that come your way, you'll learn to increasingly trust your own ability to judge their value.

Appraising Opportunities   ACTIVITY **24**

DIRECTIONS

Think of an opportunity that is before you at the present time and answer the following questions.

1. What might this opportunity give you that you don't have now?

2. Will it help you grow in new ways, or merely give you one more variation of what you already know?

3. Does it point you in the direction you want to be heading?

4. Does it pique your curiosity about something you haven't previously considered?

5. What are the trade-offs if you take this opportunity? What will you gain? What will you have to sacrifice? Are the trade-offs worth it?

6. If you don't grab this opportunity, what will you potentially miss?

7. If this opportunity doesn't seem to be worthwhile, based on how you've answered the questions so far, why are you drawn to it?

To better illustrate how you can explore your opportunities, I've included some vignettes from the work I did with a client, Mary Ann, who was sincerely interested in taking a good long look at the full range of opportunities she had open to her. Mary Ann is a thirty-one-year-old professional who works in a marketing and public relations firm. She has a degree in public relations and has worked in that field for five years. You'll see her story woven throughout this chapter.

Growing in Place

One option Mary Ann has is to remain in her present position. Like Mary Ann's, your current position may offer opportunities for growth that are worth exploring. If you enjoy your work and are satisfied with the compensation and recognition you get from it, look for possibilities to make it an even more profitable experience. To do that, adopt a "grow-in-place" strategy that will keep you on the lookout for opportunities to add value to your organization.

Start by pursuing ongoing learning and development. Commit to learning everything you can about your position and how it interfaces with other positions in your organization. Doing so will help you remain employable and improve your chances for success in your career. Do you know how your position contributes to your company's bottom line? You should. Do you know how the division you're in contributes? That's equally important. Once you know how your position and your division contribute to your company's bottom line, reach out to identify ways you can add value from within your current position and division.

Another way to grow in place is to keep your eyes open for the next big thing in your field. Hone the art of trend spotting. Do this by scanning your everyday world for information on current issues, events, products, services, and new developments. Where should you be scanning? Journals and magazines in your field are one place. But don't limit yourself. Pertinent websites, business-related newspapers and online e-zines, as well as magazines like *The Futurist, Technology Review,* and *Fast Company* can all help. Check out books that focus on futures thinking and future trends, such as *The Roaring 2000's, Blur,* and *2025.*

Keep an eye on women who are doing interesting work in your field. Communicate with them if you can (e-mail makes it easier). In addition to expanding your network, you'll probably learn about some fascinating initiatives that will keep you thriving in your field. Attend an industry-sponsored event that introduces you to some new idea or technology. Growing in place can be exciting and challenging and you don't have to move halfway around the globe to do it.

These days, a formal promotion is one possibility among many to advance in your career. With newer organizational structures looking more like webs than formal career ladders, it's possible to advance through lateral moves or even steps backward, depending on what you can learn from the move. Remember Mona from the opening section of this chapter? She transferred to another department, and in doing so gained a whole new cluster of skills she didn't have before.

Avoiding the "Doom Loop"

What if you like your field and your organization but you just can't bear the routine of your job any longer? What kinds of opportunities do you have then? Sometimes we grow restless because we're no longer challenged by our job responsibilities. We feel we're getting stale and one day is just like the next. If this sounds like your life, you may be feeling the consequences of being on the downside of the "doom loop."

The term, coined by Charles Jett and later elaborated on by Dory Hollander (1991), refers to a situation that many of us may have found ourselves in at some point in our career. The doom loop looks something like this: We take on a new job and for a while we're the "new kid on the block" who's just learning the ropes. After a period of time, we begin to feel some mastery of the skills of our job. And then, after more time has gone by, we start to get that sinking feeling that we've been doing the "same-old, same-old" for far too long. At this point, we may experience boredom and disinterest in our job. And our performance may even begin to go downhill. We begin to feel the same frustration that Charlie Jett's client did when he complained, "I'm doomed if I keep doing what I've been doing!"

Have you experienced these feelings? If you have, there is something you can do about it. You can avoid the doom loop by staying clear of the boredom and burnout. How? Continue to find new ways of doing your work or push for new learning projects that will stretch you and get you excited about growing once again.

Taking on key assignments can mean opportunities to gain new skills, get more visibility, demonstrate your talent, and position yourself for other assignments that offer increased power, responsibility, and compensation. Research by Lisa Mainiero (1994b) on executive women has shown that the ability to choose and make the best use of opportunities is often important to advancement. To seize opportunities, get clear on your strengths as well as on the general direction you want to be heading. Otherwise, you can end up accepting a lot of random assignments that don't lead in any one direction or leave you feeling scattered or dissatisfied.

In choosing assignments, be sure to consider whether the ones you're offered—or the ones you seek out—are in "career maker" departments. Gather your information, talk to your sources, and find out what possibilities the assignment really holds for getting you more of what you want from your career. Ask yourself the questions in Activity 25. If you can answer questions like these, you'll be better able to choose assignments, team spots, and similar opportunities wisely.

Taking Your Talent on the Road

If you'd really like to continue doing the kind of work you're involved in now, but you aren't really thrilled about remaining in the same organization, then another option to consider is taking your talent and experience to other organizations that are looking for your skills. Don't stop there; consider other industries than the one you're in right now.

When Mary Ann reflected on what opportunities she might pursue if she were willing to leave her company, she came up with several. She could consider PR positions in other organizations similar to the one she's in now. She could apply her talent in different industries or in non-

Evaluating Opportunities

DIRECTIONS

Think of an opportunity that is before you at the present time (the same one as for the previous activity, or a different one) and answer the following questions.

1. Does this opportunity represent a stretch for you?

2. Will you increase your skills or political acumen by taking it?

3. Whom will you have the opportunity to work with?

4. What kind of freedom will you have to call the shots?

5. What kind of support and resources will you get?

6. How will this assignment augment what you already know and position you for other advancements?

profit groups, still using the same primary skill set she's using now. Or she could explore organizations that are smaller or larger than the one she's in now. And, if she's willing to relocate, she can explore opportunities in the Pacific Northwest or the United Kingdom, geographic areas she's always been interested in. Or, she could even go back to work for a former employer, referred to as boomeranging.

Though it was once frowned on or not considered a viable option, some people are returning to companies they used to work for, and they're doing it for a number of reasons. Some return because of disenchantment with the new job that had prompted them to leave their old job in the first place; others return because of a desire to latch on to their former company's new expanded opportunities. Obviously, your ability to successfully boomerang depends on how smoothly you left your old company and what talents you can offer to get you back on the old team. But, be sure to add this option to your list of possibilities.

Reconfiguring Your Talent

Opportunities may also depend on your ability to rearrange your portfolio of talents. If you're willing to explore opportunities beyond the ones that align perfectly with a specific job title that you think you're suited for, you'll increase your opportunities exponentially. I've worked with women who, though frustrated with their current line of work, claim "There just aren't any opportunities out there." Where do they get such an idea? They get it from scanning the "Help Wanted" section of their newspaper under specific job titles, where they notice only a paltry number of listings that they aren't even interested in pursuing. But remember, the want ads account for only 5 to 15 percent of the available positions. And thinking in terms of "jobs" always limits your options.

There are a number of opportunities for demonstrating your talents in ways other than a direct match between your educational preparation and a job title. Just because you majored in accounting doesn't mean you should limit your choices to those opportunities that include the title "accountant." The same holds true for other positions. Preparation in teaching doesn't limit your options to those labeled "teacher." The same thing applies for position titles like "social worker," "systems analyst," and "engineer." It's the creative mixing of all your talents, including your formal education and training, your informal learning, your passions, your volunteer experience, and your interest in emerging fields that can be parlayed into new opportunities.

Here's the lead to a great column in *Fast Company* ("Job Titles of the Future," 1996) that asked a question and then answered it by offering some wisdom to help you reconfigure your talent.

Are You Hyphenated Enough?

The job of the future is all about hyphenates—smart people who combine education, interests, and skills to become one-person cross-functional teams. The world is no longer divided into specialists who know everything about something and generalists who know something about everything. Gaining an edge in the future depends on the ability to hone the hyphen—to creatively bundle (and re-bundle) skills and knowledge. (p. 30)

Activity 26 will help you with this.

DIRECTIONS

Get out five large pieces of paper such as newsprint or flip-chart paper, and follow the instructions for each piece in part A below.

Post these pieces of paper on a large area of wall space in a place where you can see them all at the same time, like five columns of a table.

Use another large sheet of paper and follow the instructions in part B.

Now complete part C.

See Mary Ann's lists for an example.

Part A

Sheet #1: Make a list of the skills you really enjoy using.

Sheet #2: Make a list of the positions you've held.

Sheet #3: Make a list of all your recent training, both formal and informal.

Sheet #4: Make a list of all the volunteer efforts you've been involved in.

Sheet #5: Make a list of the issues that interest you most right now.

Part B

Begin to mix up all these talents and interests—sort of a "one from column 1 and one from column 2" approach in which each sheet of paper represents a different column. Make a list of all the different ways you can "bundle" and "rebundle" yourself.

Part C

From the list you compiled in part B, select and list some creative new opportunities you could explore.

Leave your list of opportunities up in a place where you can look at it and experiment and add to it daily. Consider which opportunities this activity suggests that you might want to investigate further.

Here's just a small portion of what Mary Ann came up with and how she hyphenated herself and expanded her options.

Skills	Positions	Training	Volunteering	Interests
writing copy	advertising	business writing	newsletter for assoc.	environment
making presentations	speechwriter	Internet development	spokesperson for Sierra Club	travel
project management	asst. PR	public speaking	English skills to foreign-born women at local prison	literacy issues

Based on the list she completed in this exercise, Mary Ann determined that she could pursue positions as

- Speechwriter for heads of associations in the environmental area
- Web writer and developer for environment or travel industry
- Teacher of business writing skills
- Teacher and organizer of programs at a natural history or science museum

Remember Lalei, whose dreams of an acting career in New York didn't seem to work out? Now happily employed on the West Coast, Lalei has successfully hyphenated herself by taking her knowledge and interest in acting and entertainment, merging them with classes she took in writing code, and combining that with experience she gained in designing Web pages, to create an outstanding opportunity. She's a project manager for new websites being developed by start-ups in the entertainment field.

To truly take advantage of the widest possible range of opportunities, consider looking beyond your own field. For those who have been in low-tech fields, this may mean a move to high-tech opportunities. Much of your success at transitioning to a new career depends on your ability to identify those skills you can transfer from one field to another. And if job titles are still important to you, check the ones listed in each issue of *Fast Company*. The people and positions featured in the "Job Titles of the Future" column can get you thinking about opportunities to transfer skills you already have into positions that are being created right now—even as you're reading this page.

Shaping Your Work Life

Our new economy, driven by globalization and new technologies, has multiplied the ways we can work. For Mary Ann, these changes offer a number of opportunities for working and attending to the other priorities in her life.

- *Full-time or part-time:* Although a full-time, permanent position was once the only standard for showing a commitment to your career, that's no longer the case. True, some companies still see through only that lens. But many others are willing to consider part-time arrangements. If you've just moved to a different part of the country and you're looking for just the right position, or you're trying to finish a degree and bring in some money at the same time, it's worth your time to inquire about part-time options. These opportunities can segue into full-time work later or they can offer a style of working that best fits your needs right now.
- *Telecommuting:* Mary Ann is one of an increasing number of workers who wonder if telecommuting is a viable option. She's trying to figure out what combination of working from home and working in her office would suit her best. To make a wise choice, she first needs to know what options are available through her organization, as well as which ones they may be willing to consider. If you, like Mary Ann, are considering telecommuting for part of your work, find the best way to strike a balance between working from home and working in your office. You'll need to ask yourself questions such as, When does all the action happen for my work group? When are meetings generally scheduled? How does networking happen? How can I stay in the loop on information that may be critical to my career?

If most decisions are made and most of the strategizing and connecting takes place during the time you're off-site, then you're probably missing out on a lot of important business. One concern facing working women who are interested in experimenting with their work schedule is the issue of putting in enough "face time" to stay in the loop while attending to other dimensions of their lives. However you choose to shape your work life, it's critical that you think through all your options within the context of your life and career goals.

- *Job sharing:* Mary Ann is thinking about sharing her job with another person who is looking for part-time work right now. That would give her time to help her husband care for his elderly father. Job sharing is gaining credibility as a viable work arrangement in many cutting-edge organizations. Don't simply dismiss it or decide it's not possible in your particular position. If job sharing is an option you think would work for you, check it out.
- *Flextime:* If you know you need a flexible work schedule, find out what options you have and explore them all. To automatically dismiss any of them is to narrow your range of possibilities for creating your optimal working environment. If your organization doesn't honor flexible work arrangement requests, remember that there are a growing number of organizations that are attracting talented women by offering flextime and actually making these programs work. You probably have more options than you think.

Now take a few moments to ask yourself the questions about your work life in Activity 27.

Choosing Your Employer

When it comes to opportunities related to whom you want to work for, the new economy has turned all the old rules upside down. For Mary Ann, new workplace realities mean that she has several options. She can continue to pursue full-time employment in an organization. Or she can work as an outside consultant delivering the same kind of products and services as she is now, but doing it on her own for a number of organizations. She can also work on a project basis. Or she can work part-time for

DIRECTIONS

Answer the following questions.

1. Does the way you are working now truly suit you, given your current needs and lifestyle?

2. Does the shape of your work life support your vision of where you want to be going with your life?

3. Does your organization honor and make available a number of work arrangement options that let you do your best work?

an organization while she pursues her dream of owning and operating her own PR company during the remaining hours of the week. To consider any of these options, though, she needs to be clear about what kind of employment arrangements will make the most sense at the present time, given her current career and life goals and her other commitments and desires.

Economist Charles Handy (1990) tells us that the workforce of the future (actually it's already here) will look somewhat like a three-leafed shamrock. One leaf of the shamrock represents an organization's core workers—the qualified professionals, technicians, and managers who are essential to the organization. The second leaf represents the contract workers, those not on the organization's payroll, who do the specialized work that can be "outsourced." The third leaf represents the flexible labor force, the part-time and temporary workers.

Whichever "leaf" of the shamrock we choose, it will likely be a temporary choice that changes as our life circumstances and life goals change; this is especially so given the complexities and richness of women's lives today. Circumstances such as relocating, transitioning from school to work, or changing professions mean that a woman may very well move around among all three leaves of the shamrock, or perhaps settle into some hybrid of the three.

Consider also temping and free agent possibilities. Are you aware of organizations like M², the California-based consulting firm that will hook you up with assignments on a project basis? Have you kept up with the trends like the ones described in an article that began, "Welcome to e-lancing"? If you haven't yet discovered the possibilities for being your own boss, log on to your computer today and sites such as guru.com and freeagent.com for a whole new perspective.

How about temp work? Is your image of the temp field one of stuffing envelopes and delivering promotional literature door-to-door? If it is, then you need to raise your Awareness of the many Opportunities in the temp field. If you're a recent newcomer to the work world, temporary work opportunities can give you a chance to turn your newly minted education into dollars and experience. Or if you're a seasoned veteran, it can help you snag an interim exec position that will provide not only income but also visibility, challenge, and lots of new contacts.

Playing the Wild Cards

MARY ANN ATTENDED a weeklong seminar last month. At the seminar she met a woman from another organization who was fascinated by the projects Mary Ann has been working on. The two women exchanged business cards and promised to keep in touch. Early this morning, Mary Ann received a call from her new friend telling her about an exciting opportunity that's just opened up at her firm. She told Mary Ann she'd be perfect for the position and wondered if she'd be interested.

We can't predict opportunities that sometimes seem to come out of the blue. Wild cards show up as a new colleague we meet, a book that changes our life, an unexpected dinner we're invited to, a conference we're asked to speak at, or a mentor who presents us with a new direction we never considered before. The treasure that these events offer is the chance to turn them into opportunities.

Then there's that other class of wild cards that shows up on our doorstep. Check out Activity 28 to see how you would turn your wild cards into opportunities.

DIRECTIONS

If you woke up tomorrow morning and found that one of these events had happened while you were asleep, how would you turn your circumstances into an opportunity?

1. What if a downsizing, merger, or acquisition changed your organization into some new hybrid you couldn't even recognize?

2. What if some new technology changed the way you do your work?

3. What if there were a sudden demand for your services, way beyond your wildest expectations?

4. What if your job title became obsolete?

There's no quick or easy answer to these questions, and even though none of these scenarios is likely to greet you at 6:00 A.M. tomorrow, chances are good that some version of one of them will come knocking on your door in the not-too-distant future. How would you meet such an opportunity? With open arms and excitement? Or with your back turned quickly away? The choice is yours.

Finding Nonwork Opportunities to Learn and Grow

REMEMBER KRISTIN, the woman whose story started off this chapter? Her decision to head for Mexico may have seemed like a strange reaction to her circumstances. But Kristin had a plan. She had been studying Spanish on her own for a few years and was looking for an opportunity to learn more about Hispanic culture as well as to improve her language skills. She found a place where she could do both—an intensive month-long program in a small town that was recommended by a woman from Mexico City she had met a few years ago. She knows the experience will give her more career options internationally. Kristin will also stop in San Diego on her way home to check out opportunities for work there through some contacts she has.

Opportunities like those provided by travel or participation in volunteer efforts of your professional association often lead to possibilities you can't predict ahead of time. The trick is to view any new experience, nonwork as much as work, as an opportunity.

Making the Most of Awareness of Opportunities

Women excel at identifying opportunities, especially when we're pushed to find alternatives after a door has been closed in our face. Want a great example of such a woman? Author Dianne Hales (1999) describes the case of Mary Louise Cleave, who, as a girl, loved flying and aspired to be a stewardess. Unfortunately, because she wasn't tall enough to make the cut, she never became one. But that didn't stop opportunity-seeking Ms. Cleave. She found another employer that would let her fly. She signed on with NASA, became an astronaut, and completed several space shuttle missions.

You probably know several women among your circle of friends who are extraordinary opportunity makers—chances are good you may be one yourself. A very exciting part of being a working woman today is the chance to identify opportunities that capture our attention and passion, and then go for them. This is what pursuing work that matters is all about. This is leveraging our strengths in a workplace that truly needs what we have to offer.

What's the best way to capitalize on this Strength? Create your own opportunities. Notice what other people don't. Cash in on chances to expand your talent base. And remember, the true value of any opportunity is its ability to move you toward your best and brightest self.

CHAPTER 10

Creativity and Leadership Are the Capstone

THOUGH WE FACE unparalleled opportunities in our work world, we also face unprecedented challenges. And, in such a climate, it takes a lot more than just adjusting or tweaking our old ways of thinking and doing business to successfully accomplish the work that matters most.

If you've read through and begun to practice the other nine Strengths in this book, you've already done a great job of laying a solid foundation for your career success. Having trust in yourself, savvy about the ways of the world around you, and skill in finding and doing the work that needs doing will pave the way for you to grow professionally. In fact, if you choose to follow the suggestions and practices recommended for the first nine strengths and decide not to include Strength 10, Creativity and Leadership, in your professional development plan, you're still likely to get to most of the places you want to go in your career.

But if you are like the growing number of women I've talked with and coached who want to influence decisions about how their work is shaped and how their organizations should grow and move forward, you'll probably want to include skill in this Strength as part of your professional portfolio. Strength 10 is a capstone Strength that positions you to contribute to and influence your profession and your organization.

Setting the Stage for Using Creativity and Leadership

Before you can maximize Creativity and Leadership in your career, you'll need some prerequisites to put you on the right path. These prerequisites are (1) a Leap of Faith in Yourself, (2) a Full Measure of Courage to follow through on your ideas, instincts, and beliefs, and (3) a Commitment to Making a Difference.

In order to illustrate why faith and courage are so important to creativity and leadership, take a few moments to complete Activity 29.

Admirable Qualities   ACTIVITY **29**

DIRECTIONS

Think for a moment of three women you most admire—the ones who have made a difference in your life or in the lives of others. Picture the ones who inspire you, who motivate you to try new things or push past your self-imposed limitations. Record the names of these three women in the left-hand column below.

Now, reflect on what it is about these women that makes them such touchstones or models of excellence and inspiration for you. Write down the qualities that come to mind, as you think about each woman, in the right-hand column next to that woman's name.

Look closely at the qualities you recorded. Chances are good that, whichever qualities you listed for each woman, some element of faith and courage is woven into your entries; and these qualities are probably a good part of what makes these women the inspiration they are for you today.

Women You Admire   **Their Admirable Qualities**

1._____   _____

2._____   _____

3._____   _____

A Leap of Faith and a Full Measure of Courage are especially important in today's workplace because women who want to succeed need to be willing to literally transform themselves and their organizations. Transformation is what it will take for the modern-day pioneers who hope to lead their organizations through the complexity and changes still to come—complexity and changes that we can't even imagine today. Transformation doesn't rely on simply continuing to improve your performance or that of your company. That's critical, but it isn't enough. Transformation means opening up to a much larger view of possibilities for yourself and your organization. Activity 30 will help you open up to your transformation potential.

Your Transformation Potential ACTIVITY 30

DIRECTIONS

Answer the following questions.

1. What isn't being said or done in your profession or organization that needs to be addressed?

2. Are you, or is your profession or organization, imposing artificial barriers that limit your growth?

3. What do you have to "forget" or let go of before you can learn what you'll need for tomorrow?

4. What's your vision of personal excellence?

5. What's your vision of professional and organizational excellence?

6. What keeps you, or your organization, from moving toward it?

7. How can you, individually, and your organization reinvent yourselves daily to be all that you can be?

8. How can you link your passion with your work and leverage your knowledge more effectively?

None of these questions is easy to address. Nor can any be answered with a flip one-line solution. And bringing up questions like these won't always make you popular among your co-workers or those you report to. Yet they're some of the important questions that need to be asked for transformation to occur. To do this, you'll need enduring faith in yourself, courage, and an attitude of positive expectancy—that is, the ability to see yourself as creative, innovative, and capable of leadership in whatever position you hold and in whatever organization employs you.

Successful women who demonstrate Creativity and Leadership are those who have found issues, causes, services, or products that they believe in strongly enough to push past their fears and make a Commitment to Making a Difference. You can, too. No matter what your position in your organization or your degree of formal authority, you can make a difference. You can do it by offering your passion and skills in an environment that values them, by speaking up, and by acting on what you feel is most important.

Sara E. Melendez (1996), president of Independent Sector and board member of both Quality Education for Minorities and the National Puerto Rican Forum, is a great example of a woman who has brought Commitment to Making a Difference into her leadership role. She says,

> In retrospect, it seems that my preparation for leadership consisted of being in a series of situations where I had a strong conviction. I expressed it, and someone asked me to do something about the situation, a version of "Put your money where your mouth is." (p. 294)

To make a difference, you need to be outstanding at what you do and you need to move forward with passion and purpose. Whether you're developing a new product or service, or taking a leadership role in helping to shape a new direction for your organization, you need to know your work, your field, and the work of your organization inside and out. And for women, the requirements go even a step farther. According to Melendez,

> women and people of color also need to know a lot about the male and majority culture and styles. Outsiders, or members of minority groups seeking

entrance and acceptance into a majority culture and domain, need to be very knowledgeable about those who wield power and about the culture in which they will be working to effect change. (p. 302)

Notice she said "be knowledgeable about," not mimic. You'll lead best knowing the lay of the land but then going forward in your own way—not copying someone else's style.

The first three parts of this book offered you the building blocks for identifying and practicing the skills you'll need to accomplish the things Melendez mentions. Once you've developed some expertise, savvy, and credibility, you'll find it easier to step forward with confidence and make your voice heard.

But, in addition to knowing these external things, you'll also need to have a deep sense of who you are on the inside, along with knowing your purpose and vision. If you think this sounds similar to chapters you read earlier, you are right. Previous chapters have already raised these issues and helped you examine many of these important internal questions. When it comes to acts of Creativity and Leadership, self-knowledge becomes essential.

Daring to Stand Out

Acts of Creativity and Leadership, by their very nature, require you to stand out. And that requires you to take risks. Every woman who wants to—who dares herself to—can stand out and make a difference. You don't have to win an Olympic medal or be named Employee of the Year to qualify. "Standing out" and "making a difference" mean having the willingness to change your own life, or the lives of those you work with or serve, by virtue of how and what you choose to contribute. Offer a different perspective at a meeting when things seem stuck, take time out to listen to an employee who isn't feeling valued, or point out a better process when customer service's ratings are low and you'll help to make changes that can make a difference. You'll also get noticed because you made the effort and stuck your neck out. That ups the stakes but also multiplies your opportunities to make a difference.

Activity 31 will help you identify where you can best contribute and stand out. Your answers to these questions will give you some clues about where you can direct your time and energies to stand out and make a difference.

Are You Willing to Stand Out?   ACTIVITY **31**

DIRECTIONS

Answer the following questions.

1. What skills or talents have others encouraged you to develop or demonstrate even more than you do now?

2. What are the one or two areas of your life that you get excited about taking risks in?

3. Where in your organization or your profession do you feel it's important to add your input?

4. How can you best add that input in these areas (for example, through speaking up in meetings, serving on a committee, chairing a task force, doing research in an area that needs attention, or volunteering to serve on a community-sponsored panel)?

Focusing on What's Important

Just in case you need some reminding, you have a finite amount of energy and time to devote to your professional life. Women who make a difference—the ones who create and innovate—realize that they need to focus on the areas that are most important to them and their work. That doesn't mean you can't contribute creative ideas throughout your day. You'll probably enjoy your work even more if you can bring fresh thinking and great suggestions to it on a regular basis. But to really contribute your finest talents, you'll need to focus and follow through on the ideas, plans, and actions that mean the most to you and add the most value to your organization's bottom line.

SHARI HAS AN incredible talent for putting together proposals and possible new projects in her role in program development at the museum that employs her. Those who work with her genuinely admire her never-ending ability to come up with creative ideas to get people into the museum. But because Shari has her fingers into almost a dozen projects at any one time, she seldom has the energy or time to follow through on many of them. The result? Shari is seen as brilliant but lacking in skills to turn her ideas into realities. And, because one of the goals of her organization is to bring more people into the museum, her inability to focus and follow through keeps her from contributing to the bottom line. That perception also keeps her from moving into more senior spots at the museum.

For Shari to change the perception of others and improve her chances for career success, she'll need a clear picture of what matters most to her organization. And she'll need to focus all her efforts in that direction.

Nurturing and Supporting Your Creative Spirit

You may have heard yourself or a friend say something like, "I don't have a creative bone in my body!" If you've said this or heard another woman confess to something similar, you're not alone. Too many of us grew up in a culture that frowned on coloring outside the lines, warned against breaking the rules, and sometimes actually punished new ways of doing things—not exactly a setting that encouraged the creative spirit! And, for women, many of whom were (and still are) raised to be "good girls," the encouragement to do things differently was seldom there.

In their book *Singing at the Top of Our Lungs: Women, Love, and Creativity* (1993), Claudia Bepko and Jo-Ann Krestan write powerfully about the vital lifeblood that Creativity provides for women. They note, "Passion, love, creative expression . . . these energies are the essence of our lives. . . . to live fully, meaningfully, we need to find better access to the power to create, to share our visions, to feel deeply" (p. 255). These women make a strong case for having a system in place to nurture and support your creative spirit. Do you have support for your creative spirit? Ask yourself,

- Who encourages my Creativity?
- Who urges me forward to express myself?

If you don't have a strong network of supporters you can count on to encourage you to go for it, start today to build one. Support is especially important when you're putting yourself out there and doing things differently.

Creativity in the workplace is important for both individual workers and their organizations. On an individual level, Creativity lets us express ourselves and offer our own unique take on things. Expressing our Creativity keeps our juices flowing and our passion alive for new understandings and possibilities. If we fail to pursue and express our Creativity, we can experience a death of our spirit and a sense of disconnection from the things that keep us vital.

And, in the same way, Creativity—expressed as innovative products, processes, or services—is truly the lifeblood of a company. Unless a company can creatively differentiate itself from the competition, it will fall behind and eventually die. Creativity isn't simply a nice add-on for individuals or for organizations. Nor is it a skill that individuals can master in a half-day seminar or organizations can embrace by launching a new "Creativity initiative." Creativity is a mind-set and a daily practice. And it's an imperative in the workplace today.

"CREATIVITY IS A SOCIAL ACT. It requires an exchange between one person and another in an environment that sparks motivation. . . . With genuine care and respect for others, women can help enrich the workplace by encouraging more opportunities for skill development, increased responsibility, and appreciation of how work is valued. As workers experience success and growth in a safe, supportive, challenging environment, they are more likely to be open to expressing their ideas."
—Debora Humphreys, consultant, The Concord Group

Women have so much to contribute to the workplace when it comes to creative talent. They are participating at every level in the global rebirth that's happening today. Their ideas, discoveries, products, and services are breathing new life into organizations across every industry. Pick up just about any magazine or newspaper from *USA Today* to *Wired* to *Technology Review* and you're likely to find profiles of women experimenting, risking, and creating.

These managers, scientists, consultants, professors, artists, program developers, and leaders have all tapped into their Creativity, and they're using it to express themselves and improve their company's bottom line. Every woman can exercise Creativity in some way, and each woman who does so expands the richness and possibilities in her life and increases her likelihood of experiencing career success. Cultivating Creativity and expressing it not only increases your current job satisfaction and contribution; it's also a great extra edge when you're job seeking.

In case you're thinking that Creativity isn't already part of your portfolio, consider including instances like these:

- Each time you problem-solve on the team you've been assigned to, you're being creative.
- Each time you come up with a tailor-made solution to deal with an upset customer, you're being creative.
- Each time you step into a heated debate between two employees and suggest an agreement they both can live with, you're being creative.
- And each time you suggest a new tack when everyone else feels stuck, you're being creative.

You're probably more creative than you give yourself credit for and, if that is the case, it's important to stretch your definition of Creativity to encompass a much wider range of behaviors. Do this and you'll give yourself permission to think bigger, get more playful, and see a much broader range of options.

How can you start becoming more creative in your everyday routine? Begin by recognizing and honoring your creative talents. Here are some suggestions to get you started.

- Let go of the notion that Creativity is a gift given to a few select people, such as artists, actors, and leaders of companies. Creativity is a gift that lives at the core of every one of us. Learning more about that gift will give you the ability to express it.

- Take the time to find your own creative "tools"—those things that let you express yourself most fully. Tools can be a paint brush, a lump of clay, a knack with words, the ability to see texture, the art of noticing commonalities between people who are in conflict, or the ability to describe a vision of the future like no one else can. Give yourself permission to explore who you are and discover what pleases you. We each have a spark of Creativity.

- Refuse to censor yourself or give your efforts short shrift. Creativity flourishes only when it's nourished and honored.

- Realize that Creativity is a process, not an event. As such, it needs to be nourished and practiced over time.

- Watch out for busyness—often the enemy of the creative process. If you're constantly on the go, don't expect to get in touch with your Creativity. The muse doesn't usually show up when your mind is full of "stuff." Give yourself and your Creativity a place and time to breathe.

- Don't be concerned about the final product of your efforts. Likewise, don't worry about whether there's a connection between your creative efforts and your workday responsibilities. There doesn't need to be one. By encouraging the creative process, you'll bring this gift with you into your professional life, no matter what your job title or duties.

- The next time you face a problem at work, hold off looking for solutions immediately. Practice playing with the problem and invite others in your work group to do so as well. Opportunities like these are a great way to put your Creativity to work.

Thinking and acting creatively opens new possibilities in all areas of your life. You're likely to see patterns you have never noticed before or come up with ideas seemingly out of the blue. Opening the door to your creative self also opens the door to new possibilities in all areas of your life.

Embracing a New Model of Leadership

No doubt about it, the times we're living in are extraordinary. Never before in our history have we had access to so much information, such technological power, such a lightning-fast communication network, and so many opportunities to form alliances on a global scale. How does one best lead in such a world? In some situations, we have to make it up as we go along; in others, we need to explore alternative ways of thinking and acting to accomplish business goals. That's because models that were built on old rules and protocols don't usually apply to the rapidly changing world that greets us each day. And while that can be frightening to some, it can be exhilarating to others who are willing to take chances and try out new possibilities. Are you one of those women?

If you were to travel back in time—say twenty years or so—and take a look at the Leadership model of the day, you'd probably notice that it relied a lot on hierarchy. Most vital information was entrusted to a few top leaders who decided when, where, how, and with whom to share it. That model had a lot in common with the military model of the time, in which a few people in charge of the thinking issued orders to the many people in charge of the doing. Because of the speed at which things moved back then, there was generally sufficient time for the people at the top to make the business decisions and pass them down the organizational chart until word was spread to all the "troops." The troops then could begin implementing whatever actions were called for.

Now, leave that scene and fast-forward to the workplace you walk into each morning. How effective do you think that old Leadership model would be today? How would it stand up against the realities you see around you? And what's your guess on how effective that model would be tomorrow? If your answer is "zip," you're right. Even if your organization is still trying to lead in that way, chances are it will change in the very near future—or it won't even be around to wonder what went wrong.

Remember that old standard refrain for why women weren't ready for Leadership roles? The prevailing view—not that long ago—was that women didn't have "enough time in the pipeline." That view is a product of an old-style economy that no longer makes much sense. As Harriet Rubin (2000) points out, "Forget the old argument that women haven't invested generations in business. . . . In the new economy, everybody was born yesterday" (p. 252). The bottom line these days is that Leadership calls for new models and new approaches that are more in tune with the times. The challenge for women today is to let go of whatever limiting personal beliefs or cultural messages they may hold about what it takes to be a leader. Do that and you'll have a lot more energy and space to create your own version of what a leader can look like in this new economy.

Because successful organizations are heading more in the direction of flatter hierarchies, advancement and Leadership opportunities don't proceed in a neat sequence of moves up an invisible pyramid-like organizational chart. Responsibility, decision-making ability, and clout these days have less to do with rank, title, or a corner office. And they have much more to do with your ability to shape the work and influence the direction of your organization from whatever position you hold—while motivating those around you to take risks and add value every single day.

Given the complexity of today's workplace, these are no simple feats. You can't rely on the old rules or a cushion of time to sort things out. That's why the faith and courage mentioned at the start of this chapter are so essential.

Recognizing the New Leaders

Leaders today—and those just emerging—embody the qualities discussed in this chapter, and more. They're the ones who act powerfully in the present while keeping an eye on the next big thing of the future. If you want to see some of the women who are leading in this way, begin noticing the ones who are embracing the cutting edge and turning their businesses into exciting enterprises, such as those in the following examples.

ANITA BORG is variously described as a Silicon Valley superstar, a brilliant computer scientist, and an advocate for women who is leading a worldwide movement to redesign the relationship between women and technology. What is it that makes Anita such a legendary leader? It's her vision, her courage, and her real Commitment to Making a Difference. Add to this the fact that she's chosen to put her talent into one of the biggest forces shaping our world today—technology—and you can see how she manages to excel.

RADHA BASU, CEO of Support.com, is another leader who's dancing on the cutting edge. She's found a way to succeed by leveraging technology and women's strengths. Says Basu (quoted in Compton, 2000), "The whole Internet phenomenon is very customer-focused. And one of the things about women is that we're able to look at customer needs, be appreciative of them, and develop cooperative, win-win relationships" (p. 1).

CHRIS TURNER, an executive with the job title of "Learning Person" for Xerox Business Services, says her job is "to disturb the system. I give people new ways to think" (quoted in Webber, 1996, p. 113). Turner's style emphasizes empowerment and she gives us one more example of a woman making a difference in a way that works for her—and adds value to her organization at the same time.

These three brief profiles highlight the fact that women are stepping up and leading with a clear picture of who they are and how and what they want to contribute. Their words and their work are great examples of why you, too, must know yourself and what you want to contribute. Why not push your boundaries to see what Leadership you're capable of? Here are some suggestions to help you move toward Leadership roles.

SUGGESTIONS AND STRATEGIES

- Read about, talk to, and follow the careers of women like Borg, Basu, and Turner— as well as leaders you've gotten to know personally. The more you know about and connect with such women, the more you'll learn about a wide range of Leadership models—and the more you'll see yourself as a potential leader, as well.

- Carry an unconditional, unwavering belief in yourself and your talents with you wherever you go.

- Make full use of everything you learn and leverage it to add value.

- Embrace the latest information and technology.

- Your particular take on things is valuable. Be willing to express it.

Developing Your Leadership Potential

If you're sincere about wanting to lead others, you'll first need to know yourself. Successful, committed leaders know themselves well; they know where they're headed; and, though they may not be sure of their exact route, they stay focused on their own "true north" and keep moving in that direction. And they make sure the direction they're heading in is one that truly matters to them.

Would you like some proof of the value of self-knowledge and commitment in nourishing your Leadership potential? Here are some words of wisdom from Arlene Blum (quoted in Barre, 1998), the mountain climber who led the first woman-only climb to the summit of Annapurna and a presenter at executive leadership programs. When asked what she thought separated people who make it to the top from those who don't, she responded,

> The real dividing line is passion. . . . As long as you believe that what you're doing is meaningful, you can cut through fear and exhaustion and take the next step. . . . If you can't picture it, you won't make it. To get anywhere—in climbing or in business—you have to know where you're headed. I'm not talking about "corporate vision." I'm talking about a clear picture that depicts where you, the individual, want to go. (p. 72)

Part One of this book focused on just these qualities in the personal resilience strengths. Before you attempt to influence your organization, it would be worth your time and effort to review the questions raised there about who you are and what you like about yourself.

Once you have that self-knowledge, you'll find it easier to lead with your strengths, and doing so will help you excel. Our strengths are frequently in areas that we most enjoying using. It feels good to contribute our best efforts knowing we'll shine. It works for us and for our organizations. And it helps when we're responsible for leading others. Are you intimately familiar with the areas in which you shine?

Before going any farther, you may want to stop here long enough to reflect on your particular strengths. The questions in Activity 32 will help you summarize what you've learned about yourself so far and can help you highlight some of your strengths, which, in turn, can suggest your Leadership capabilities.

Your Leadership Potential ACTIVITY **32**

DIRECTIONS

Answer the following questions.

1. Based on what you've learned about yourself in practicing the other nine Strengths, where do your greatest talents lie?

2. Assuming you can get whatever training or education you need to bring yourself up to where you need to be in your areas of interest and expertise, where could you make the most difference? What activities, causes, roles, types of organizations, or industries would you feel most excited about contributing to and taking on more visible assignments in?

3. What is it that you do that says "yes" to your heart—and feels right while you're doing it?

4. In what issues, topics, or areas of your work do you really want to take on higher levels of responsibility?

5. In what areas of your work do others look to you for guidance, direction, or answers?

6. In what one or two areas of your work could you secretly claim to be a guru? (Don't worry, you needn't proclaim this in the company newsletter—just reflect on those areas in which you feel particularly pleased with your own abilities).

After you have completed Activity 32, look back at your answers. Chances are good that your responses contain several clues to the arenas in which you have Leadership potential.

Taking on a formal Leadership role is one way to shape policy and direction for your organization. Here are some suggestions for ways to work toward formal Leadership roles.

- Discuss Leadership opportunities with a mentor, trusted boss, or senior-level woman you admire. Ask her opinion about how best to move into Leadership roles.

- Volunteer for Leadership opportunities through your professional association.

- Take the lead or the chair in the next project or committee you're placed on.

- Get feedback on your Leadership style from someone you trust.

- Inquire about Leadership development programs in your organization, professional association, or community.

Becoming an Everyday Leader

Leadership skills can be honed daily, regardless of your position. Your attitude and your willingness to think like a leader prepare and position you for spots with more influence and decision-making responsibility. Activity 33 will help you see how you can use Leadership abilities every day.

Everyday Leaders   ACTIVITY **33**

DIRECTIONS

Answer the following questions.

1. Do you have deep knowledge about your organization?

2. Do you know the abilities of those around you?

3. How can you influence the way work is done in your unit or your organization?

Organizations on the cutting edge, and smart enough to make the most of their human capital, will nurture multiple forms of Leadership and different types of power in every one of their employees. The challenge to you is to determine what kind of Leadership role you want to take on and how best to move toward that goal. If you make the mistake of believing that power and Leadership can only come from certain people who have been "anointed" to lead, you're selling yourself short. If your vision is that small—or if your organization is that shortsighted—both you and it will lose out on your Leadership potential and talent. A larger vision calls for seeing yourself as a leader each and every day, and a farsighted organization will support that vision.

Here's one more reason for practicing everyday Leadership: Careers, job titles, position responsibilities, and even organizations seem to be continuously "shape-shifting" these days. Leadership roles and responsibilities are also shifting. The person who led a project last month may be a team member on another project next month. Someone you worked for in another organization may report to you now. In an environment like this, Leadership becomes more fluid. If you can practice thinking like a leader and hone your skills every chance you get, you'll find that your Leadership capabilities will benefit you in just about any workplace situation.

Making the Most of Creativity and Leadership

Here are some strategies that will let you capitalize even more on Creativity and Leadership. Weave these ideas into your workplace repertoire and you'll make yourself even more valuable to your organization.

SUGGESTIONS AND STRATEGIES

- *Become increasingly techno-savvy.* Women who are the most successful leaders understand that technology, itself, isn't the name of the game. It's the tool that lets you into the game. To make the most of Strength 10, as well as the other nine, you need to be more than computer literate—that implies only a minimum level of skills. Technological savvy means you know the computer-related tools and language of your industry and your organization. If it's a piece of software used to manage projects, capture information, or update a client's account—know how to use it. If it's language that everybody around you uses to discuss a particular project, product, or service—understand that language.

In addition to seeing technology as a tool, consider it a field you may want to investigate further. Science, engineering, and technology are wide-open fields where women are currently underrepresented; these areas are the ones destined to explode in growth in the days ahead. As Anita Borg reports, "Technology is going to change our political, economic, social, personal lives. Women need to be there saying, 'This is how we want things to change.'" Check out groups like Systers (www.systers.org/mecca), a global electronic network of women in computer science and technology.

- *Align your personal passions with your organization's goals.* This may seem like a no-brainer, but don't underestimate its importance. Passion is the fuel that will let you step forward and contribute your best effort. If your passion and your organization's direction don't seem to be going down the same track, your chances (and your desire) to contribute and lead will be diminished.

- *Think like a futurist.* Act in the present, but keep a constant eye on the future, scanning the horizon for trends. Reflect on their possible meaning for you and your organization and consider how you can capitalize on them. Play out different scenarios. Ask yourself some *"what if?"* questions. *What if* things in your organization or your industry continue going the way they are? *What if* a competitor comes along and changes everything? *What if* you could take your organization in a whole new direction? *What if* you took that senior spot? How would you do things differently?

- *Seek out role models and sources of inspiration in unlikely places*—or at least not in the usual places you might go to for guidance. Search out artists, read the diaries of women pioneers, find women whose perspectives are different from yours. Pay attention to the ideas of women outside your industry or profession. They are often the ones who can teach us the most.

- *Cultivate a global mind-set.* The future belongs to those who can see, appreciate, and learn from a myriad of perspectives and worldviews. If you take the time to learn about another's culture, chances are good you won't be able to go back to seeing in a more limited way again. Each time we step outside the boundaries and limits we've imposed on ourselves, we grow. So does our Leadership capability and so does our organization.

CHAPTER 11

Planning for Success Puts Your Strengths to Work

NOW THAT YOU'VE had the opportunity to read through the Four Themes and the Ten Strengths That Matter Most, you're ready to capitalize on them by shaping your career in ways that will make a difference to you—and to your organization.

Where do you start? Just as you learned in Strength 4 (Knowledge, Skills, and Learning), the best way to profit from Knowledge and make it work for you is to apply it to your life circumstances and begin to take action on it.

With these points in mind, I invite you to use this final section as an opportunity to begin to make some changes in your professional life and move toward healthy career success. The following section offers suggestions and guidance in crafting a Development and Action Plan that will work best for you.

The purpose of the plan is to

- Move you closer to your image of your best and brightest self
- Help you succeed in your career in healthy ways
- Give you a road map you can use immediately

The focus of the plan is on

- *Development:* Identifying the best possible ways you can continue to grow professionally—wherever you are in your career right now
- *Action:* Putting your plan to work, beginning today

There are three different ways you can design a plan for yourself. Depending on the time and energy you have right now—and the other commitments and responsibilities in your life—you'll want to choose a plan that fits you and sets you up for growth and success. Read over the three variations that follow and turn to the pages that contain the plan that fits for you right now.

- *The Go-for-It-Immediately Development and Action Plan:* This is for you if you know just where you want to begin and how you want to go about it. Pages 214–217 will guide you in putting your plan into action.
- *The Quick Development and Action Plan:* If you can't take the time for or make the commitment to a more thorough review of the Ten Strengths, this simplified plan can provide enough structure to get you rolling. Pages 218–219 will give you what you need.
- *The In-Depth Success Plan:* If one of your top priorities at the present time is professional development and career advancement, this more detailed plan will probably work best for you. With it, you can take all you've learned throughout this book and design a detailed, personally tailored plan for yourself. Pages 220–243 will guide you.

The Go-for-It-Immediately Development and Action Plan

This plan is for you if you know just where you want to focus your time and energy right now. Choose the one or two Strengths that you really want to work on. Turn back to the chapters for the Strength(s) you've identified and look over the exercises or special sections or notations you made. These particular pages will give you some ideas about how to begin. Record your information in the spaces below.

1. FIRST STRENGTH I WANT TO WORK ON RIGHT NOW

The way I'll begin to work on it

Resources I'll use to help me

----

2. SECOND STRENGTH I WANT TO WORK ON RIGHT NOW

The way I'll begin to work on it

Resources I'll use to help me

Set a date (perhaps one month from now) to use as a checkpoint to measure your progress. On that date (mark it in your planner so you don't forget), complete the following sentences.

Progress Review Date _____

I'm using this Strength right now when I

_____

_____

_____

The barrier(s) I've encountered in trying to work on this Strength are

_____

_____

_____

The ways I've overcome these barriers are

_____

_____

_____

If you haven't been successful in overcoming a barrier, you just need to identify other ways to reach your Development and Action Plan goals. Complete the following sentences.

In order to get past barriers that keep me from making full use of this Strength, I'll need

----

One other way I can choose to work on this Strength is

The way I believe my work on this Strength is helping me advance my career is

----

To further capitalize on this Strength, I'll need

The Quick Development and Action Plan

If you're interested in working on your professional development right now, but time and life commitments make it hard for you to take on anything new, this plan will let you determine areas which will give you the quickest return on your investment.

Look over your scores from the Ten Strengths That Matter Most Inventory and complete these two sentences.

The Strength I scored highest on is

The Strength I scored lowest on is

For each of these Strengths, determine one action you could take, beginning tomorrow, that would help you capitalize on the Strength more than you are right now.

For your highest-scoring Strength, consider possible actions that would let you further demonstrate your uniqueness or expertise.

Strength --

Action --

Resources I need to help me take that action

For your lowest-scoring Strength, consider possible ways to try something new regarding this Strength. Be careful, though, not to push yourself so far that you'll feel uncomfortable making the effort, give up, or decide it's too much of a hassle to give it a try.

Strength --

Action --

Resources I need to help me take that action

Now, look at your Theme scores and complete the following questions

The Theme I scored highest on --

The Theme I scored lowest on --

Ask yourself how you could give more attention to your lowest-scoring Theme. In answering this question, think small. What can you do simply that will enable this Theme to work better for you?

Ask yourself how you can revel even more in the Theme that you scored highest on. How can you further enrich your life or your career—or simply celebrate the fact that you're already doing well on this particular Theme?

The In-Depth Success Plan

For this in-depth plan, you'll need time to review each Strength in more detail. When working on the following sections, complete as many questions as you are comfortable doing at one time. Try to completely finish the Strength you're working on before you set your plan aside. Work on the questions when you're feeling fresh—not when you're exhausted. Your answers will be much more valuable and useful to you if you've worked on them when you're energized.

To get the most from this plan, give yourself sufficient time to consider each of the questions in the sections that follow. Also, set yourself up for success by designing a plan that you'll feel motivated to follow through on. Consider getting together with other women to form a Career and Life That Matters Most support group. Meet on a regular basis to encourage one another in making your plan a reality.

This in-depth plan will ask you to list certain action items related to each Strength, so you'll want to have a picture in mind of just what it is you want to work on to further capitalize on each Strength. To put this plan to work for you, you'll also need to determine specific ways you'd like to practice each Strength. You may find that in some Strengths, a shift in your attitude or perspective will make a difference. For other Strengths, trying out a new behavior may make the difference in your career or life.

In addition to knowing what it is you'd like to do differently, you'll also need to consider the specific situations in which you want to practice your new attitude, perspective, or behavior. Here are some examples of situations in which you could practice increasing your use of a particular Strength.

- In your work as part of a team you're on
- In a current routine assignment you're working on
- In a new assignment you've just been given
- In materials you write
- In presentations you make
- In speeches you give
- In your interactions with a particular co-worker

- In a new or existing mentoring relationship you're part of
- With a specific client or customer you're serving
- In a professional association you belong to
- In the contributions you make at staff meetings
- In reports you put together
- In nonwork activities you participate in
- In the way you begin or end your day

Strength 1: Confidence

Feelings of self-esteem and belief in one's ability to succeed in job- and career-related tasks

KEY POINTS

- A woman's sense of self-esteem and confidence affects every aspect of her career.
- It's vital to "set yourself up" for success by reflecting on past successes and by holding affirming, appropriate, and realistic expectations of yourself when you're taking on new challenges.
- Career encouragement is essential. Get it often and from several different sources.
- One of today's major "confidence challenges" for a woman centers on her ability to believe in herself enough to take on more visible positions and higher-risk assignments.

QUESTIONS

1. From my reading and reflecting, what points stand out for me about CONFIDENCE?

----

2. I already use CONFIDENCE now when I

----

3. How would *further* increasing my use of CONFIDENCE make a difference *in my career or in my life overall*?

----

4. How would *further* increasing my use of CONFIDENCE make a difference *to my organization*?

----

5. What is one specific area of my daily life in which I could increase my use of CONFIDENCE?

----

6. Specifically, what will I do to increase my strength in CONFIDENCE in this particular area of my work/life? (*For instance, what attitude or behavior will I try out?*)

----

7. What resources do I need to be able to carry out this action? (*For instance, time, education, training, coaching, support of a person you report to, co-worker, colleague, friend or partner, reading materials, etc. Make certain that you can access or seek out the resources you need to be able to carry out your action. Otherwise, you'll feel frustrated when you hit a roadblock*).

----

8. How will I know that I've succeeded in increasing my use of CONFIDENCE? What will be different?

Strength 2: Self-Reliance

Sense of inner direction and trust in oneself

KEY POINTS

- A focus on Self-Reliance, rather than control, is needed in today's workplace.
- A focus on the work that needs doing, rather than on your job description, can make you more employable.
- "Free agent" status should be cultivated, no matter who you are working for.
- One of today's major Self-Reliance challenges is to become more comfortable relying on yourself and your resources.

QUESTIONS

1. From my reading and reflecting, what points stand out for me about SELF-RELIANCE?

----

2. I already use SELF-RELIANCE now when I

----

3. How would *further* increasing my use of SELF-RELIANCE make a difference *in my career or in my life overall*?

----

4. How would *further* increasing my use of SELF-RELIANCE make a difference *to my organization*?

----

5. What is one specific area of my daily life in which I could increase my use of SELF-RELIANCE?

----

6. Specifically, what will I do to increase my strength in SELF-RELIANCE in this particular area of my work/life? (*For instance, what attitude or behavior will I try out?*)

----

7. What resources do I need to be able to carry out this action? (*For instance, time, education, training, coaching, support of a person you report to, co-worker, colleague, friend or partner, reading materials, etc. Make certain that you can access or seek out the resources you need to be able to carry out your action. Otherwise, you'll feel frustrated when you hit a roadblock*).

----

8. How will I know that I've succeeded in increasing my use of SELF-RELIANCE? What will be different?

Strength 3: Planfulness and Initiative

Developing an open-ended plan and taking action
to move toward a desired future

KEY POINTS

- Planfulness and Initiative are complementary: Planfulness is shaping the path, Initiative is taking it.
- The ability to shape a career plan today is crucial, but it needs to be open-ended and flexible.
- True Planfulness cannot be done without (1) reflecting on core questions about how you want to shape your life, and (2) assessing your skills and identifying what you need to be able to move toward your vision of a life that truly matters to you.
- Women already demonstrate Initiative. Today's major challenge is to choose when, where, and how best to step forward to demonstrate one's talents.

QUESTIONS

1. From my reading and reflecting, what points stand out for me about **PLANFULNESS** and **INITIATIVE**?

----

2. I already use **PLANFULNESS** and **INITIATIVE** now when I

----

3. How would *further* increasing my use of **PLANFULNESS** and **INITIATIVE** make a difference *in my career or in my life overall*?

----

4. How would *further* increasing my use of **PLANFULNESS** and **INITIATIVE** make a difference *to my organization*?

----

5. What is one specific area of my daily life in which I could increase my use of **PLANFULNESS** and **INITIATIVE**?

----

6. Specifically, what will I do to increase my strength in **PLANFULNESS** and **INITIATIVE** in this particular area of my work/life? (*For instance, what attitude or behavior will I try out?*)

----

7. What resources do I need to be able to carry out this action? (*For instance, time, education, training, coaching, support of a person you report to, co-worker, colleague, friend or partner, reading materials, etc. Make certain that you can access or seek out the resources you need to be able to carry out your action. Otherwise, you'll feel frustrated when you hit a roadblock*).

----

8. How will I know that I've succeeded in increasing my use of **PLANFULNESS** and **INITIATIVE**? What will be different?

Strength 4: Knowledge, Skills, and Learning

Demonstrated expertise and a commitment
to professional development

KEY POINTS

- Remaining on your own cutting edge is essential.
- Benchmarking your own Knowledge and Skills is one way to stay current.
- You need to identify Learning opportunities and position yourself to take advantage of them.
- Professional development is a 24/7 activity. It can be done through work and nonwork activities.

QUESTIONS

1. From my reading and reflecting, what points stand out for me about **KNOWLEDGE, SKILLS,** and **LEARNING**?

----

2. I already use **KNOWLEDGE, SKILLS,** and **LEARNING** now when I

----

3. How would *further* increasing my use of **KNOWLEDGE, SKILLS,** and **LEARNING** make a difference *in my career or in my life overall*?

----

4. How would *further* increasing my use of **KNOWLEDGE, SKILLS,** and **LEARNING** make a difference *to my organization*?

----

5. What is one specific area of my daily life in which I could increase my use of **KNOWLEDGE, SKILLS,** and **LEARNING**?

----

6. Specifically, what will I do to increase my strength in **KNOWLEDGE,**
    SKILLS, and **LEARNING** in this particular area of my work/life? (*For*
    instance, what attitude or behavior will I try out?)

----

7. What resources do I need to be able to carry out this action? (*For*
    instance, time, education, training, coaching, support of a person
    you report to, co-worker, colleague, friend or partner, reading mate-
    rials, etc. Make certain that you can access or seek out the resources
    you need to be able to carry out your action. Otherwise, you'll feel
    frustrated when you hit a roadblock).

----

8. How will I know that I've succeeded in increasing my use of
    KNOWLEDGE, SKILLS, and **LEARNING**? What will be different?

Strength 5: Interpersonal Competence

Ease in relating to others and the ability to nurture and maintain relationships over time

KEY POINTS

- Women's strength in relationship building is a key competency in today's global workplace.
- Just because relational skills are essential today doesn't mean they are always recognized and valued. Get whatever support you need to demonstrate your relational skills.
- Networking and mentoring activities today are different from older, more rigid versions. These activities should be tailored to fit your current needs.
- Today's mentoring and networking challenge is to identify and use options for connecting that provide ongoing support and advancement and that work for a woman's busy life.

QUESTIONS

1. From my reading and reflecting, what points stand out for me about INTERPERSONAL COMPETENCE?

----

2. I already use INTERPERSONAL COMPETENCE now when I

----

3. How would *further* increasing my use of INTERPERSONAL COMPETENCE make a difference *in my career or in my life overall*?

----

4. How would *further* increasing my use of INTERPERSONAL COMPETENCE make a difference *to my organization*?

----

5. What is one specific area of my daily life in which I could increase my use of **INTERPERSONAL COMPETENCE**?

----

6. Specifically, what will I do to increase my strength in **INTERPERSONAL COMPETENCE** in this particular area of my work/life? (*For instance, what attitude or behavior will I try out?*)

----

7. What resources do I need to be able to carry out this action? (*For instance, time, education, training, coaching, support of a person you report to, co-worker, colleague, friend or partner, reading materials, etc. Make certain that you can access or seek out the resources you need to be able to carry out your action. Otherwise, you'll feel frustrated when you hit a roadblock*).

----

8. How will I know that I've succeeded in increasing my use of **INTERPERSONAL COMPETENCE**? What will be different?

Strength 6:   Flexibility and Savvy

Changeability with a practical understanding of the dynamics of an organization and the ability to effectively present and position oneself and one's work within it

KEY POINTS

- Many women are skilled at being flexible in their personal lives, but they don't always know how best to capitalize on this Strength in their professional lives.
- There are times when a woman needs to guard against being too flexible.
- The old perception of Savvy as "playing office politics" is out of step with the times. Savvy is about knowing how work gets done effectively inside an organization.
- Flexibility and Savvy both require you to pause, understand what's going on around you, and determine how best to respond to the situation.

QUESTIONS

1. From my reading and reflecting, what points stand out for me about **FLEXIBILITY** and **SAVVY**?

----

2. I already use **FLEXIBILITY** and **SAVVY** now when I

----

3. How would *further* increasing my use of **FLEXIBILITY** and **SAVVY** make a difference *in my career or in my life overall*?

----

4. How would *further* increasing my use of **FLEXIBILITY** and **SAVVY** make a difference *to my organization*?

----

5. What is one specific area of my daily life in which I could increase my use of FLEXIBILITY and SAVVY?

----

6. Specifically, what will I do to increase my strength in FLEXIBILITY and SAVVY in this particular area of my work/life? (*For instance, what attitude or behavior will I try out?*)

----

7. What resources do I need to be able to carry out this action? (*For instance, time, education, training, coaching, support of a person you report to, co-worker, colleague, friend or partner, reading materials, etc. Make certain that you can access or seek out the resources you need to be able to carry out your action. Otherwise, you'll feel frustrated when you hit a roadblock*).

----

8. How will I know that I've succeeded in increasing my use of FLEXIBILITY and SAVVY? What will be different?

Strength 7: Balance

The ability to lead one's life with attention to wholeness and harmony

KEY POINTS

- Balance is a lifelong endeavor and usually doesn't respond to "quick-fix" solutions.
- Every woman's formula for Balance will be different, and it will change based on the circumstances of her personal and professional life.
- The blurred boundaries between your workplace and your personal life can be a source of stress unless the situation is monitored.
- The nonwork aspects of your life should not be simply time that you're not working. They should be cultivated and enjoyed for all the other dimensions of life they let you express.

QUESTIONS

1. From my reading and reflecting, what points stand out for me about BALANCE?

----

2. I already use BALANCE now when I

----

3. How would *further* increasing my use of BALANCE make a difference *in my career or in my life overall*?

----

4. How would *further* increasing my use of BALANCE make a difference *to my organization*?

----

5. What is one specific area of my daily life in which I could increase my use of BALANCE?

----

6. Specifically, what will I do to increase my strength in BALANCE in this particular area of my work/life? (*For instance, what attitude or behavior will I try out?*)

----

7. What resources do I need to be able to carry out this action? (*For instance, time, education, training, coaching, support of a person you report to, co-worker, colleague, friend or partner, reading materials, etc. Make certain that you can access or seek out the resources you need to be able to carry out your action. Otherwise, you'll feel frustrated when you hit a roadblock*).

----

8. How will I know that I've succeeded in increasing my use of BALANCE? What will be different?

Strength 8: Coping and Self-Care

The ability to use self-nurturing strategies to maintain health and well-being at work and in one's personal life

KEY POINTS

- Coping and Self-Care are not luxuries. They are keys to lifelong health and well-being.
- Putting Coping and Self-Care "on hold" indefinitely can result in burnout and exhaustion.
- Practicing Coping strategies is a first step toward a healthier lifestyle.
- Weaving nurturing, Self-Care behaviors into your life is the next step toward creating a healthy life and careers.

QUESTIONS

1. From my reading and reflecting, what points stand out for me about COPING and SELF-CARE?

----

2. I already use COPING and SELF-CARE now when I

----

3. How would *further* increasing my use of COPING and SELF-CARE make a difference *in my career or in my life overall*?

----

4. How would *further* increasing my use of COPING and SELF-CARE make a difference *to my organization*?

----

5. What is one specific area of my daily life in which I could increase my use of COPING and SELF-CARE?

----

6. Specifically, what will I do to increase my strength in COPING and SELF-CARE in this particular area of my work/life? (*For instance, what attitude or behavior will I try out?*)

----

7. What resources do I need to be able to carry out this action? (*For instance, time, education, training, coaching, support of a person you report to, co-worker, colleague, friend or partner, reading materials, etc. Make certain that you can access or seek out the resources you need to be able to carry out your action. Otherwise, you'll feel frustrated when you hit a roadblock*).

----

8. How will I know that I've succeeded in increasing my use of COPING and SELF-CARE? What will be different?

Strength 9: Awareness of Opportunities

Being alert to opportunities and able to capitalize on them

KEY POINTS

- There has been an explosion in the number of opportunities available in the workplace, but women are not always aware of the full range of options open to them.
- Opportunities encompass several dimensions including the place you can work, the ways you can demonstrate your talent, the ways you can advance your career and the work/lifestyle you can create for yourself.
- Shaping the best possible career today must begin with an assessment of all the opportunities open to you.

QUESTIONS

1. From my reading and reflecting, what points stand out for me about **AWARENESS OF OPPORTUNITIES**?

----

2. I already use **AWARENESS OF OPPORTUNITIES** now when I

----

3. How would *further* increasing my use of **AWARENESS OF OPPORTUNITIES** make a difference *in my career or in my life overall*?

----

4. How would *further* increasing my use of **AWARENESS OF OPPORTUNITIES** make a difference *to my organization*?

5. What is one specific area of my daily life in which I could increase my use of AWARENESS OF OPPORTUNITIES?

----

6. Specifically, what will I do to increase my strength in AWARENESS OF OPPORTUNITIES in this particular area of my work/life? (*For instance, what attitude or behavior will I try out?*)

----

7. What resources do I need to be able to carry out this action? (*For instance, time, education, training, coaching, support of a person you report to, co-worker, colleague, friend or partner, reading materials, etc. Make certain that you can access or seek out the resources you need to be able to carry out your action. Otherwise, you'll feel frustrated when you hit a roadblock*).

----

8. How will I know that I've succeeded in increasing my use of AWARENESS OF OPPORTUNITIES? What will be different?

Strength 10: Creativity and Leadership

> The ability to see oneself as a leader with the skills,
> talent, and insight to successfully move oneself
> and one's organization into the future

KEY POINTS

- Never before have women had the preparation, the skill set, the experience, and the opportunity to make such a difference; and their contribution is definitely needed in today's global workplace.
- You must trust yourself and gather the courage you need to make a difference in the way that only you can.
- You demonstrate Creativity each time you do something in a way that is unique to you and your perspective.
- You don't have to lead, but the workplace and your own life will be all the richer if you do.

QUESTIONS

1. From my reading and reflecting, what points stand out for me about CREATIVITY and LEADERSHIP?

----

2. I already use CREATIVITY and LEADERSHIP now when I

----

3. How would *further* increasing my use of CREATIVITY and LEADERSHIP make a difference *in my career or in my life overall*?

----

4. How would *further* increasing my use of CREATIVITY and LEADERSHIP make a difference *to my organization*?

----

5. What is one specific area of my daily life in which I could increase my use of **CREATIVITY** and **LEADERSHIP**?

----

6. Specifically, what will I do to increase my strength in **CREATIVITY** and **LEADERSHIP** in this particular area of my work/life? (*For instance, what attitude or behavior will I try out?*)

----

7. What resources do I need to be able to carry out this action? (*For instance, time, education, training, coaching, support of a person you report to, co-worker, colleague, friend or partner, reading materials, etc. Make certain that you can access or seek out the resources you need to be able to carry out your action. Otherwise, you'll feel frustrated when you hit a roadblock*).

----

8. How will I know that I've succeeded in increasing my use of **CREATIVITY** and **LEADERSHIP**? What will be different?

As you continue to work on and revisit your plan, it's a good idea to jot down notes that capture some of the things you've accomplished and the confidence and increased satisfaction you're feeling in your career. Use the lines below to record these successes along the way. Why not jot them down at the end of each workweek?

Week 1

Week 2

Week 3

Week 4

When you reach a point at which you feel you've accomplished as much as you'd like to in your plan, take some time to congratulate yourself and celebrate. Then, when you're feeling the urge to look at your career and life goals once again, return to this last chapter and determine which other Strengths you'd like to direct your attention to next.

Here's to a successful and meaningful life that truly works for you!

Concluding Thoughts

Women *do* have what it takes to succeed in healthy ways. And we *can* make a tremendous difference in the workplace and in our own lives. I grow more convinced of that every time I speak to a group of women or talk to a group of decision makers inside cutting-edge organizations.

By far the greatest gift we can offer ourselves and our organizations is the recognition of the value that we bring with us. Ultimately, I believe it's the uncovering of our strengths—not the hiding or the covering over of our weaknesses—that lets us succeed.

I wish you courage and faith and a future full of passion and possibilities as you create a life and a career that matter most to you.

Caitlin Williams

Bibliography

Adler, N. (1997). Global leadership: Women leaders. *Management International Review, 37,* 17.

American Association of University Women. (1999). *Gaining a foothold: Women's transitions through work and college.* Washington, DC : Author.

Bandura, A. (1997). *Social learning theory.* Englewood Cliffs, NJ: Prentice-Hall.

Bandura, A. (1977). Self-efficacy: Toward a unifying theory of behavioral change. *Psychological Review, 84,* 191–215.

Bender, S. (1995). *Everyday sacred.* New York: HarperCollins.

Bepko, C., and Krestan, J. A. (1993). *Singing at the top of our lungs: Women, love, and creativity.* New York: HarperCollins.

Betz, N. (1992). Counseling uses of career self-efficacy theory. *Career Development Quarterly, 41,* 22–26.

Bliss, W. (1999). Why is corporate culture important? *Workforce* [online]. www.workforceonline.com.

Bravo, E. (1995). *The job/family challenge: A 9 to 5 guide.* New York: John Wiley & Sons.

Bridges, W. (1997). *Creating you & co.* Reading, MA: Addison-Wesley Longman.

Bridges, W. (1994). *Jobshift.* Reading, MA: Addison-Wesley Longman.

Brown, J. (1994). Finding her here. In S. Martz (Ed.), *I am becoming the woman I've wanted.* Watsonville, CA: Papier-Mache Press.

Brown, T. (1996, September). Pursuing the protean employee. *Management Review, 86,* 24–25.

Catalyst. (1999). *Creating women's networks*. San Francisco: Jossey-Bass.

Catalyst. (1998). *Advancing women in business*. San Francisco: Jossey-Bass.

Challenger, J. (1998, January–February). Future career: Director of socialization. *Futurist, 32*(1), 2.

Clarke, J., Kole, J., and Williams, C. (1997). Mentoring: Models and benefits for women's management and leadership development. In American Society for Training and Development, *Issues and Trends Report*, pp. 1–4. Alexandria, VA: American Society for Training and Development.

Comeau-Kirschner, C., and Wah, L. (2000, January). Who has time to think? *Management Review, 89*, 16–23.

Compton, M. (2000). It's about relationships. *Salon Technology* [online]. http://www.salon.com/tech/view/2000/oz/zz/basu/index.html.

Drucker, P. (1999, March–April). Managing oneself. *Harvard Business Review, 77*(2), 65–74.

Fletcher, J. (1999). *Disappearing acts: Gender, power and relational practice at work*. Cambridge, MA: Massachusetts Institute of Technology.

Galinsky, E. (1999). *Ask the children: What America's children really think about working parents*. New York: William Morrow.

Gardner, M. (1998, January 15). Brown baggers mix briefcases and child concerns. *Christian Science Monitor, 13*, 12.

Hackett, G., and Betz, N. (1981). A self-efficacy approach to the career development of women. *Journal of Vocational Behavior, 18*, 326–339.

Hakim, C. (1995). *We are all self-employed: The new social contract for working in a changing world*. New York: John Wiley & Sons.

Hales, D. (1999) *Just like a woman*. New York: Bantam Books.

Hall, D. T. (Ed.). (1996). *The career is dead, long live the career.* San Francisco: Jossey-Bass.

Hallowell, E. (1999, January). The human moment at work. *Harvard Business Review, 77,* 58.

Hammond, K. (2000, December). Work and life—Helen Wilkinson. *Fast Company, 30,* 188.

Handy, C. (1990). *The age of unreason.* Boston, MA: Harvard Business School Press.

Helgesen, S. (1999). Women as leaders: Masters of the value of change. Keynote Speech at American Management Association Executive Forum on Women in Management, Chicago.

Helgesen, S. (1998). *Everyday revolutionaries: Working women and the transformation of American life.* New York: Doubleday.

Helgesen, S. (1996). Leading from the grass roots. In F. Hesselbein, M. Goldsmith, and R. Beckhard (Eds.), *The leader of the future,* pp. 19–24. San Francisco: Jossey-Bass.

Hollander, D. (1991). *The doom loop: A step by step guide to career mastery.* New York: Penguin Group.

HR Career Center (2000). [online]. http://www.hrplaza.com/hrcareer-center/.

Job titles of the future (1996, August/September). [column]. *Fast Company, 4,* 30.

Judy, R., and D'Amico, C. (1997). *Workforce 2020: Work and workers in the 21st century.* Indianapolis: Hudson Institute.

Kane, K. (1996). Are you hyphenated enough? *Fast Company, 4,* 30–32.

Krueger, P. (1999, November). Betrayed by work. *Fast Company, 29,* 182–196.

La Barre, P. (1999). What's new, what's not. Unit of one. *Fast Company, 21,* 73.

La Barre, P. (1998). Here's how to make it to the top. *Fast Company, 17,* 72.

Levoy, G. (1997). *Callings.* New York: Harmony Books.

Listen up. (1999, June 28). *Time, 153,* 25.

Madden, K. (2000). *How to turn a place around: A handbook for creating successful public spaces.* New York: Project for Public Spaces, Inc.

Mainiero, L. (1994a). On breaking the glass ceiling: The political seasoning of powerful women executives. *Organizational Dynamics, 22*(4), 4–21.

Mainiero, L. (1994b). Getting anointed for advancement: The case of executive women. *Academy of Management Executive, 8,* 84–86.

Martz, S. (Ed.). (1994). *I am becoming the woman I've wanted.* Watsonville, CA: Papier-Mache Press.

Maslach, C., and Leiter, M. (1997). *The truth about burnout.* San Francisco: Jossey-Bass.

McCauley, L. (1999). Next stop—the 21st century. *Fast Company, 27,* 108.

McCune, J. (1999, October). Sorry, wrong executive. *Management Review, 2*(89), 16.

McQueen, A. (1999, June 11). Debt blocks some women from college. [online] www.womwneCONNECT.com.

Melendez, S. (1996). An outsider's view of leadership. In F. Hesselbein, M. Goldsmith, and R. Beckhard (Eds.), *The leader of the future.* San Francisco: Jossey-Bass.

Mieszkowski, K. (1999, September). Report from the future: The ex-files. *Fast Company, 27,* 52–54.

Mieszkowski, K. (1998a). Careers—Eunice Azzani. *Fast Company, 20,* 128.

Mieszkowski, K. (1998b). Sisterhood is digital. *Fast Company, 27,* 198.

Mitchell, K., Levin, A., and Krumboltz, J. (1999). Planned happenstance: Constructing unexpected career opportunities. *Journal of Counseling and Development, 77,* 115–124.

Pelton, J. N. (1998). The fast-growing global brain. *Futurist, 33*(99), 24.

Peters, T. (1999a). *The brand you 50*. New York: Alfred A. Knopf.

Peters, T. (1999b) *The project 50*. New York: Alfred A. Knopf.

Pfeffer, J., and Sutton, R. (2000). *The knowing-doing gap*. Boston: Harvard Business School Press.

Porter, S., Porter, K., and Bennett, C. (1999, May 2). Be your own boss, even if you work for someone else, you're in charge of your career. *National Business Employment Weekly, 18*, 11–12.

Quinn, J., Anderson, P., and Finkelstein, S. (1996). Managing professional intellect: Making the most of the best. *Harvard Business Review, 74*(2), 71.

Rice, V., and Stackpole, B. (1995, November 13). Charm school. *PC Week, 12*(45), 1–5.

Row, H. (1998). Coping—Martin Seligman. *Fast Company, 20*, 196.

Rubin, H. (2000, January–February). Living dangerously. *Fast Company, 31*, 248–252.

Sax, L. J., Astin, A. W., Korn, W. S., and Mahoney, K. M. (1998). *The American freshman: National norms for fall 2000*. Los Angeles: Higher Education Research Institute, UCLA.

Scott, J., and Hatalla, J. (1990). The influence of chance and contingency factors on career patterns of college educated women. *Career Development Quarterly, 39*, 18–30.

Seligman, M. (1990). *Learned optimism*. New York: Pocket Books.

Siebert, K. (1996). Experience is the best teacher, if you can learn from it. In D. T. Hall (Ed.), *The career is dead, long live the career*. San Francisco: Jossey-Bass.

Siegel, M. (1998, November 9). The perils of culture conflict. *Fortune, 1*, 257.

Sinetar, M. (1988). *Elegant choices, healing choices*. Mahwah, NJ: Paulist Press.

Snelling Personnel Services website [online]. www.snelling.com.

Society for Human Resource Management. (1999). *Research: Barriers to advancement survey.* Alexandria, VA: Author.

Spreitzer, G., and Quinn, R. (1996). Empowering middle managers to be transformational leaders. *Journal of Applied Behavioral Science, 32,* 237–261.

Sullivan, K., and Mahjalik, J. (2000, Winter). Increasing career self-efficacy for women: Evaluating a group intervention. *Journal of Counseling & Development, 78,* 54–62.

Ten major trends for 1999. (1998, December 10). *Trend Letter, 24*(17), 2.

Tharenou, P., Latimer, S., and Conroy, D. (1994). How do you make it to the top? An examination of influences on women's and men's managerial advancement. *Academy of Management Journal, 37,* 899–931.

U.S. Department of Labor, Women's Bureau, Facts on Working Women [online]. http://www.dol.gov/dol/wb/public/wb_pubs/hot2000.html.

U.S. Department of Labor, First National Working Women's Summit [online]. http://www.dol.gov/dol/wb/public/wb_pubs/97sum.html.

Valian, V. (1998). *Why so slow?: the advancement of women.* Cambridge, MA: Massachusetts Institute of Technology.

Wacker, W., and Taylor, J. (2000). *Visionary's handbook.* New York: HarperCollins.

Wacker, W., and Taylor, J. (1997). *The 500 year delta.* New York: HarperCollins.

Watch out for promotion potholes. (1999). *Career Confidential, 2*(119), 1–2.

Webber, A. (1996). XBS learns to grow (Interview with Chris Turner). *Fast Company, 10,* 113.

Weil, M., and Rosen, L. (1997). *TechnoStress.* New York: John Wiley & Sons.

Williams, C. (1999). Reconnecting with nature in the third quarter. *Career Planning and Adult Development, 15,* 121–127.

Williams, C. (1998, November 1). Job success in the global economy. *National Business Employment Weekly, 17,* 44.

Williams, C. (1997, June 22) Succeeding as an executive temp. *National Business Employment Weekly, 16,* 11–14.

Williams, C. (1996a). Balance at midlife: Finding the road back to ourselves. *Midlife Woman, 5,* 1–6.

Williams, C. (1996b, November 10). Job-search advice for women candidates. *National Business Employment Weekly, 15,* 9–10.

Williams, C. (1995). Career at midlife, opportunities and challenges. *Midlife Woman, 4,* 1–5.

Williams, E., Soeprapto, E., Like, K., Touradji, P., Hess, S., and Hill, C. (1998). Perceptions of serendipity: Career paths of prominent academic women in counseling psychology. *Journal of Counseling Psychology, 45*(4), 379–389.

Young, M. (1996). Career issues for single adults without dependent children. In D. T. Hall. (Ed.), *The career is dead, long live the career.* San Francisco: Jossey-Bass.

Index

opportunities, 238–239; Planfulness, 57; professional role, 35–36; Savvy, 112, 115, 232–233; Self-Care, 236–237; self-efficacy, 27–28; Skills, 62, 80, 228–229; Strengths, 10–17, 50–51, 61–62; techniques for, 80

Self-Care: activities for promoting, 166; assessments of, 236–237; definition of, 18; focus of, 159; key points of, 236; practicing of, 170–171

self-confidence. *See* Confidence

self-doubt, 23

self-efficacy: assessment of, 27–28; career development effects, 26; definition of, 25; high levels of, 26

self-esteem: accomplishments, 25; basis of, 24; building of, 23–25; low levels of, 24

self-expectations: assessment of, 30–31; high level of, 30–31

self-identity, 141–143

self-image: assessment of, 35–36; challenging outdated views, 37

self-knowledge: Creativity and, 198–199; Leadership and, 208; of Strengths, 50–51; value of, 208

self-put-downs, 35

Self-Reliance: assessments of, 40–43, 224–225; career decisions based on, 44–46; control and, 47–49; definition of, 17; description of, 39–40; example of, 43–44; free agency, 46; importance of, 40; key points of, 224; strategies for, 52–53; Strengths and, 50–51; support network, 52; work focus effects, 51

self-responsibility, 44–46

self-trust, 50–51

Seligman, Martin, 48–49

Siebert, Kent, 89

Sinetar, Marsha, 153

Skills: benchmarking of, 81–83; communication, 97–99; definition of, 18,

228; developmental assignments, 87–88; education for increasing, 84–87; key points of, 228; performance appraisals for assessing, 83; professional development plan, 90; relational, 94–96; requirements for maintaining, 91; self-assessment of, 62, 80, 228–229; speaking, 98–99; statistics regarding, 75; strategies for, 91–92; training opportunities for increasing, 87; updating of, 77; valuing of, 76–77

speaking skills, 98–99

Strengths: Big Picture, 18; Career Enhancement, 18, 73–74; Confidence-related, 29–30; Inner Resilience, 17–18; Quality of Life, 18; self-assessment of, 10–17, 50–51, 61–62; self-knowledge of, 29, 50–51; situations for practicing, 220–221; success plan for developing. *See* success plan; types of, 8. *See also* specific strength

stress: anticipating of, 163–165; personal, 161–162; proactive approaches for handling, 164–165; work-related, 160–161

success: definition of, 3; language of, 113–114; methods for achieving, 23; plan. *See* success plan; support network and, 171–173

success plan: focus of, 213–214; go-for-it immediately, 214–217; in-depth, 220–243; purpose of, 213; quick development, 218–219; Strengths assessment. *See* self-assessments

support network: creative spirit and, 201–202; self-reliance benefits of, 52; success and, 171–173

talents: creative, 204; leaving organization to expand, 184–185; reconfiguring of, 186–189

Taylor, Jim, 58, 71, 109

techno-savvy, 211–212

technostress, 163

telecommuting, 189

temp work, 192

Tharenou, Phyllis, 33

thinking: actions initiated after careful thinking, 69; flexible, 116–117; futurist, 212

timing, 180

training, 87

transformation of self, 197

trend spotting, 182

uncertainty: goal setting in times of, 64–65; planning for, 58–59

vacation, 170

vision, 62–63

Wacker, Watts, 58, 71, 109

weaknesses, 29

Weirich, Wendy, 145

Williams, Elizabeth, 179–180

women: barriers for, 4; role and responsibilities, 4. *See also* self

work: balancing of, 141–143; boundary setting, 143–144; finding work that needs to be completed, 43, 63–64; stress associated with, 160–161

work life, 189–190

workplace: changes in, 3–4; creativity in, 202; future trends in, 191

yourself. *See* self